# THE AMATEUR ZOOLOGIST'S GUIDE
# TO TURTLES AND CROCODILIANS

# THE AMATEUR

# ZOOLOGIST'S

*Color photos on jacket front:*
*Bog Turtle – author*
*American Alligator – Z. Leszczynski*

# GUIDE TO TURTLES AND CROCODILIANS

by

Robert T. Zappalorti

Stackpole Books

THE AMATEUR ZOOLOGIST'S GUIDE TO TURTLES AND
CROCODILIANS

Copyright © 1976 by
Robert T. Zappalorti

Published by
STACKPOLE BOOKS
Cameron and Kelker Streets
Harrisburg, Pa. 17105

Printed in the U.S.A.

**Library of Congress Cataloging in Publication Data**

Zappalorti, Robert T.
  The amateur zoologist's guide to turtles and crocodilians.

  Bibliography: p.
  Includes index.
  SUMMARY: An introduction to the identification, behavior,
characteristics, and ecology of various species of crocodiles and
turtles.
  1. Turtles—Juvenile literature. 2. Crocodiles—Juvenile
literature. [1. Turtles. 2. Crocodiles] I. Title.
QL666.C5Z33      598.1'3      75-44169
ISBN  0-8117-0097-6

*To my wife Letty and our four children: Debbie Ann, Kelly Ann, Robert Thomas and Michael James, with love and affection.*

# CONTENTS

# Appendixes

# ACKNOWLEDGMENTS

W hen I first decided to write this book, with some prompting by friends, I knew it wasn't going to be an easy task. I did not realize, however, that it would be so time consuming and so large an undertaking as it turned out to be. Many unforeseen problems came up during the long preparation of the text, and the help and encouragement of many good friends and colleagues enabled me to complete the task. It is to these people that I am deeply indebted—for their help, thoughtfulness, and fine advice.

Special thanks is due to Robert Scott for initially encouraging me in the project. He also helped me work out its outline and format and served as my field editor as well.

Special gratitude is extended to Messrs. Peter Brazaitis of the Department of Herpetology at the New York Zoological Society (Bronx Zoo), and Wayne Frair, professor of biology at Kings College, Briarcliff Manor, New York. Both of these men are authorities in their respective fields and acted as my technical advisors and scientific editors. Peter Brazaitis, who is an expert on crocodilians of the world, supplied literature and other data and he also read the chapter on alligators and crocodiles, and made several important suggestions. Wayne Frair generously provided data and pictures of the rare leatherback sea turtle, as well as scientific papers, and he reviewed the text on turtles.

A number of other friends and professional herpetologists offered a variety of favors for which I am also grateful. These include the loan or gift of herpetological papers and living specimens for photographic purposes; the review of portions of the text; and help in collecting data and living specimens. These include: Dr. James D. Anderson, John L. Behler, Tom J. Bloomer, J. Kevin Bowler, Robert L. Brander, Dr. Richard C. Bruce, Dr. Charles J. Cole, Margaret Coleman, David Collins, Dr. Roger Conant, Dr. Herndon G. Dowling, Arsene Eglis, Georg Zappler, Dr. Max Hecht, Ernst G. Hofmann, Richard Holub, the late Carl F. Kauffeld, Phil Kearney, Andrew Koukoulis, Gopher Kuntz, Marty Kupersmith, Harvey Langabeer, Ken Nemuras, Marilyn Nicholas, George Porter, George Psaltis, Ben Sanders, Fred Stolle, William Summerville, Russell Urso, Dr. Phillip C. Walker, Steven Weinkselbaum, Dr. Paul Wohl, Letitia R. Zappalorti, and Dr. Richard G. Zweifel.

Illustrations, diagrams and line drawings were provided by Florence Bramley, Florence Gibson, and Paul Connor.

Although I provided many of the photographs that appear in this book, I also had to rely heavily on friends and colleagues for additional ones. I am especially grateful to my good friend and long time collecting colleague, Saul Friess, for encouraging me to write this book and for teaching me how to use a camera. I am also grateful for the cooperation and generosity of such talented photographers as: Andrew Koukoulis, Zigmund Leszczynski, Jack Muntzner and Manuel Rubio.

I also wish to express my deepest gratitude and appreciation to Elaine Cohen, and Chris M. DeFranco for their helpful suggestions and encouragement, and for the tedious job of typing the manuscript.

Finally, I am indebted to my good friend, co-worker and longtime associate, Edward Johnson, for assisting in a variety of ways. Ed helped with the research on the tuatara and crocodilian chapters and the bibliography.

ROBERT T. ZAPPALORTI

# INTRODUCTION

Herpetology, the study of reptiles and amphibians, is a subject that has become increasingly popular in recent years. This growing interest is due to the changing attitudes of the public toward the outdoors and the study of nature, including herptiles. Years ago, most people were not familiar with such words as ecology, erosion, food chain or natural habitat. But today, with all of the exposure that the natural sciences have received on television and in the movies, these have become household words. Educators are making use of large numbers of herptiles in their science classes and laboratories and are teaching young people that snakes and other reptiles are beneficial animals that play an important part in the balance of nature. During my twelve years of service at the Staten Island Zoo, I have personally seen a great expansion in the interest that people have for reptiles and amphibians. Many herptiles are now common pets and can be purchased in most pet stores across the country.

Attention to herpetology, however, varies widely, falling into several categories. There are the professional herpetologists who make their living working directly with reptiles and amphibians. Of the professionals, the most obvious are those people who work in zoos and museums; the zoo directors, curators and reptile keepers, the museum curators and technicians. These people have a responsibility to show or exhibit local and exotic forms of reptiles and amphibians to the general public. An important part of their job is making people aware of the useful functions these animals have and the role they play in the delicate balance of nature.

The not-so-obvious professional herpetologists are the university professors, field ecologists and scientists who carry on research in the field and in the laboratory, studying the behavior and life histories of the herptiles. Largely due to their efforts, we now better understand the basic biology of reptiles and amphibians and the interaction and interrelationships among them and their environment.

Then there are the amateur herpetologists, the people who find herptiles interesting, and in some cases, fascinating. These are the collectors and hobbyists who keep a few "herps" in their home terrariums. Most amateurs tend to focus on one group of reptiles or amphibians. Some prefer keeping snakes; others prefer lizards or turtles. The boa constrictor, iguana or baby turtle purchased at a local pet shop, or the garter snake or toad found in the backyard is what stimulates a person's curiosity at the start. Once a liking for these animals is developed, one's enthusiasm for herpetology grows.

This book is intended to provide the amateur herpetologist with scientific information that is easily understood; however, the professional may also find it informative. Much data is included about each family, genus and species so as to provide an adequate background for the naturalist to be able to identify properly the crocodilian or turtle found or observed. It also provides enough information so that there is a better understanding of the behavior and needs of these animals. If the location is known from which a particular reptile was collected, the type of habitat in which it lived, the average daily temperature of its environment, and the foods it ate in the wild, better care can be taken of the herptile in captivity. By simulating its needs as if it were in the wild, it can be kept more successfully in a home enclosure by the amateur herpetologist.

Zoology, biology and ecology students will find the information in this book helpful also. I have tried to use the most up-to-date herpetological nomenclature. The common and scientific names are based on the list published in 1956 by the American Society of Ichthyologists and Herpetologists in their journal, *Copeia*. Many of these names have been changed, however, since the publication of that list, so I have followed the usage of names published in the second edition of Roger Conant's *Field Guide to Reptiles and Amphibians of Eastern and Central North America.*

With this book, the amateur naturalist will become familiar with the behavior, breeding habits and characteristics of most United States crocodilians and turtles. Wherever possible, I have recounted the life history of those that I personally have studied in the field and laboratory and added observations and anecdotes from my many field experiences.

# Chapter 1

# INTRODUCTION TO REPTILES

A reptile (Class Reptilia), by definition, is a vertebrate animal occupying a position more advanced than fishes and amphibians, but lower on the scale of animal life than the birds and mammals.

In all reptiles the skin is covered with dry scales or horny plates. They breathe air with well-developed lungs and cannot physiologically produce their own body heat like birds and mammals can, for they are "cold-blooded". Reptiles reproduce by means of internal fertilization. They lay tough, leathery-shelled eggs on land, or give birth to young by retaining eggs inside their bodies until they are ready to hatch as live young. They do not lay eggs in the water as most amphibians must. Their young emerge from the eggs looking like miniature replicas of the adults and they have much the same behavioral activities.

Of all the creatures that still survive on the earth today, only five main groups of backboned animals fall into this category.

These are: crocodilians, turtles, lizards, snakes, and the little-known, rare lizardlike creature called the tuatara.

These modern-day reptiles are most numerous in the tropical and semitropical countries around the world. Some reptiles can survive in climates with very cold winters by hibernating in fizzures or burrows well below the frost line. Others live in dry, sandy desert regions around the world and are able to survive by alternately seeking cooler places in which to hide during the day and warmer places at night. During prolonged hot or dry spells, they remain burrowed in the ground where some moisture is present, or buried beneath dried mud. This is called estivation.

## HISTORY OF THE REPTILES

The early "stem" reptiles evolved from amphibian ancestors during a period in time which paleontologists—scientists who study extinct animals—call "the Permian," which closed the Paleozoic era. It was during that period, some 235 million years ago, when the reptiles replaced the amphibians as the dominant animals. Their great success was partially due to the fact that their amphibian ancestors evolved the use of internal fertilization and eventually were able to lay shelled eggs on land. They were now free from breeding in water as their ancestors did. The highly specialized, shelled eggs evolved slowly over the years. Theoretically, the long process probably went something like this: during one of the long droughts when the waters were receding, one or more species of amphibian laid eggs that were able to withstand slight drying out. These species survived and their egg-laying abilities became stronger and eventually led to a strain whose eggs could resist evaporation for much longer periods of time. In the generations that followed, selective breeding favored the amphibians that laid eggs with thicker, tougher coverings. Eventually, these animals could lay their eggs on land without fear of their drying out because a system of membranes had developed inside the thin shells which guarded the embryo that was completing its development within. The creatures that hatched from such eggs were the "stem" reptiles, (Cotylosauria), born ready for life on land and resembling their parents in appearance and habits. As their fossil remains have shown, these reptiles were highly successful organisms and they became abundant and diverse. Reptiles eventually occupied every type of habitat niche, virtually throughout the world.

This was the beginning of a new era in ancient times, one which the paleontologists call the "Mesozoic era." It was during the early Mesozoic—the Triassic period, more than 185 million years ago—that the reptiles branched out into many diverse forms. Some dominated the land, such as the orders Ornithischia and Saurischia (commonly called the dinosaurs), while others of the order Sauropterygia took to the sea where they dominated as fierce predators of fishes and smaller reptiles. A few reptiles of the order Pterosauria, mastered the ability to fly, and they flew through the air in search of their prey long before the appearance of the "warm-blooded" birds.

By mid-Mesozoic times—the Jurassic period—the reptiles had reached their "Golden Age," for they now dominated the earth and continued to do so for the next few million years until the end of Mesozoic era (the Cretaceous period). At that time, the dinosaurs began to disappear with bewildering abruptness. The reasons for their sudden decline are poorly understood by paleontologists. The fossil history that has been pieced together shows only that the reptiles vanished quickly. Many theories have been offered to account for it, but none has been scientifically proven.

The "Golden Age of Reptiles" ended with the close of the Cenozoic era, the "Age of Mammals" was just beginning. With the disappearance of the dinosaurs and their relatives, it wasn't long before the mammals filled the empty gaps in the environment. Their chance to dominate had come at long last, and the stage was now set for the long, slow evolution of man. The only reptilian survivors are crocodilians, turtles, lizards, and snakes, and the tuatara. It is these present-day reptiles with which I am mainly concerned, and only the kinds that are known to occur in the United States. A short text is included on the tuatara, because of its importance to herpetology and its uniqueness as the species that is the sole living representative of the Rhynchocephalians, an ancient order of reptiles whose ancestors can be traced back in time for some 200 million years.

# TUATARA
*(Sphenodon punctatus)*

The tuatara, *Sphenodon punctatus*, is a lizardlike reptile found only on tiny islands off the coast of New Zealand. It is a member of the "beak-headed" group of reptiles, and is often referred to as a "living fossil." A living fossil can be defined as any species of animal that has survived unchanged, from an evolutionary standpoint, over a period of millions of years. The beak-headed reptiles were thought to have been extinct for at least 100 million years, but in 1831 a living tuatara was discovered in New Zealand.

### Size and Body Structure

Tuataras are stout, heavy-bodied reptiles. Each individual possesses a row of spines down the center of its back and tail. The males grow to a length of about two feet and a weight of two pounds; females average much shorter and weigh only about half as much. Although the tuataras resemble lizards, they are distinctly different from them. One major difference is the absence of a penis in male tuataras. Another important difference is in the structure of the skull, which is more primitive than in modern lizards.

Another interesting aspect of the tuatara is its possession of a third or parietal "eye." This "eye," complete with lens, retina, and nerve leading to the brain, is situated at the center of the head and is probably used to differentiate between light and dark, since it cannot perceive images. The tuatara also provides us with a rare example of a reptile with a true voice. In its natural environment it can often be heard croaking on cool, misty nights.

### Coloration

These are drab, brownish-olive reptiles, but with a yellow spot in the center of each scale. The young tend to be far more colorful with a prominent pattern of white and grayish stripes under the head and a few light, transverse bars on the abdomen. This juvenile pattern is lost with age.

### Range

The tuatara is only found on about twenty islands off the New Zealand coast. It also occurred on the two main north and south islands, but was quickly exterminated with the introduction of European civilization.

*A lone tuatara, Sphenodon punctatus, emerges from its daytime retreat to begin foraging for food. They often share the same burrow with birds, especially the Petrel, (seen flying in the background). Their range is restricted to a number of islands off the coast of New Zealand. On cool, misty nights their croaking voice can sometimes be heard.*

### Breeding Habits

Only recently have the breeding habits of *Sphenodon* been observed both in the field and in the laboratory. Early summer, which is from November to January in New Zealand, is the mating and egg-laying season. The incubation period of the tuatara's eggs is about thirteen months, far longer than any other reptile.

In most cases mating takes place in early summer. Insemination is accomplished by means of simple cloacal apposition, a far less sophisticated method than among the other reptilian orders. Females deposit eight to fourteen elongated, hard-shelled eggs in a shallow depression about four or five inches deep. The yellowish-white eggs measure about one and three-sixteenth of an inch in length and are about ½ inch wide. They are usually covered by the female with sand or other loose material. The nest-chamber is dug well away from the home burrow where the eggs can be warmed by the heat of the sun. The developing embryo makes considerable progress in the warm summer months, but as the cooler weather arrives, the process slows down drastically. During the winter, the egg-embryo of *Sphenodon* hibernates and continues to develop slightly in the spring. However, in the second summer, the embryo apparently lies dormant and goes through an apparent estivation period until just before the end of the incubation period. The tough, leathery shell is cut by a horny egg-tooth that is located on the tip of the snout of the young tuatara, but this is lost within a week or so. Incidentally, the tuatara requires about twenty years to achieve sexual maturity. This has led some herpetologists to estimate the potential life span of a tuatara to be 100 years or more.

### General Discussion

The tuatara is an interesting animal. In its natural habitat, it lives in close association with several species of birds. One type, a petrel, digs a burrow in which to lay its eggs. *Sphenodon* will often share the burrow with the petrel, feeding on the insects attracted by the bird's droppings. It also has been known to feed on petrel eggs and chicks, but this is not a common occurrence. The tuatara sometimes shares a burrow with another type of bird called the sooty shearwater. One reason why this relationship seems to work well is because the bird is out of its burrow fishing during the day while *Sphenodon* sleeps, and the tuatara forages for food at night while the bird sleeps.

Since tuataras are so rare, they are fully protected by the New Zealand government. A person going on to an island where tuataras are found must have a permit and he is not allowed to handle or molest the animal in any way. It has been estimated that there are about 10,000 tuataras living today, and only a very small number of these are allowed to be exported to zoos and museums around the world. At the time of this writing, there are about twenty-four tuataras in eight different zoos. Sixteen of these specimens are in zoos in Australia and New Zealand. Tuataras are difficult to keep alive in captivity because of the special conditions they require. Besides being nocturnal, they have temperature requirements that are unusual for a reptile. In fact, they have been reported to be active at temperatures as low as 45° F.

J. Kevin Bowler, Curator of Reptiles at the Philadelphia Zoo, reports receiving a pair of tuataras as a gift to his institution from the New Zealand government. Attempts are being made to breed them in captivity, but first the zoo had to meet certain strict requirements for housing the reptiles. One provision was to provide an air-conditioned cage that would match the temperature, humidity and day-night cycle of the New Zealand climate. Another requirement was that the adult tuataras could not be placed on exhibit. So far the tuataras have been doing well in their cage and have adjusted to captivity. We may hope that the Philadelphia and other zoos are successful in their endeavor to breed this unique reptile, for it would indeed be a shame if some day in the future the tuatara was known only from preserved specimens in museums or pictures in a textbook.

# Part I
# CROCODILES

# Chapter 2

# INTRODUCTION TO CROCODILIANS OF THE UNITED STATES

$\text{T}$he crocodilians (Order Crocodilia) include the alligators, caimans, crocodiles, and the gavial. They are large reptiles with elongated bodies and snouts, a compressed tail and two pairs of short legs. All of the crocodilians are placed in the order Crocodilia, and are grouped in three families:

1. ALLIGATORIDAE: The American and Chinese alligators and South American caimans. Seven species are known.
2. CROCODYLIDAE: The crocodiles and the false gavial. Thirteen species.
3. GAVIALIDAE: The gavial. One species.

The crocodilians are widely distributed throughout the tropical and subtropical regions of the world including Africa, Asia, Australia, North America, and South America.

## EVOLUTION

The crocodilians are the only living representatives of the subclass Archosauria. This subclass also includes such extinct forms as the dinosaurs, pterosaurs (flying reptiles), and the ancestors of modern birds. The first appearance of the crocodilians took place in the upper Triassic period, and although they were less specialized than some of the other reptiles in this group, they survived to the present day while the others became extinct. For this reason the crocodilians are often referred to as "last of the ruling reptiles."

## GENERAL DISCUSSION

What is the difference between an alligator and a crocodile? If there is any one question which I am asked the most, this has to be it. When I was a keeper going about my duties in the alligator pool at the Staten Island Zoo, it was inevitable that one of our visitors would ask this question. Since it is a source of confusion for the amateur, let me answer correctly. The most noticeable difference between the alligators and crocodiles is the shape of the head. Alligators have broad, rounded snouts whereas most crocodiles, notably our American crocodile, have narrow snouts that taper to a point. This difference is not so noticeable in hatchlings and very young specimens. One sure identifying clue is the difference in the arrangement of the teeth. Although both

Photo by Manuel R

*The American alligator, Allig*
*mississippiensis, has a bl*
*rounded snout, and most of*
*lower teeth are not visible w*
*the mouth is closed—but they*
*quite noticeable once the mc*
*is open.*

*uvenile American alligator.*

the alligator and crocodile have a large fourth tooth on each side of the lower jaw, the alligator possesses a special socket for that tooth in the upper jaw so that when the mouth is closed no teeth are visible. Crocodiles do not have the fourth tooth hidden, and it shows on the outside edges of the upper jaw, presenting a fierce appearance even with the mouth closed.

The last difference is one which most persons are not likely to know, but one to which most reptile keepers will readily attest. In disposition, most crocodiles are far more aggressive than alligators.

On one occasion at the famed Ross Allen Reptile Institute at Silver Springs, Florida, I was visiting my friend, Andrew Koukoulis who was then Curator of Reptiles. Andy had to retrieve a dead rabbit from the cage of a six and a half-foot mugger crocodile, *Crocodylus palustris,* a native of India, Pakistan, and Ceylon. Although Andy had a three-foot long pair of "Pilstrom tongs," he couldn't quite reach the rabbit and had to enter the cage to remove the refused food. Keeping his eyes on the crocodile at all times, he picked up the rabbit and dangled it in front of the

crocodile in a last attempt to get it to take the food. Quite uncharacteristically, the crocodile did not react.

At that rebuff, Andy handed me the tongs and the rabbit so he could climb out. Throughout his entire stay in the cage his eyes had been riveted on the crocodile, alert for the least sign of movement. Now he had to turn quickly, grasp the rail and lift himself over the fence. The moment that he did, the crocodile lunged and snapped. It seemed to be aware of its best advantage and took it without hesitating, the moment Andy was not looking. Fortunately, Andy was too quick for the "croc" and was over the fence before it got near him.

Peter Brazaitis, Assistant Animal Manager at the Bronx Zoo in New York, has developed sexing techniques for crocodilians as well as a key for identifying the twenty-one living species. He is but another expert who will attest to the potentially dangerous

Photos by the au

*In contrast to alligators, the American crocodile, Crocody. acutus, has a narrow, tape. snout with the fourth tooth of lower jaw exposed when mouth is closed. When the poir mouth is open, the teeth noticeably longer than those the gator.*

nature of many true crocodiles as opposed to the American alligator. However, Pete does not consider most crocodilians to be any significant threat to man, even in the wild.

According to Kevin Bowler, Curator of Reptiles at the Philadelphia Zoo, a small crocodile of about six feet is capable of jumping three feet off of the ground. Though the legs are short, the powerful tail is used in conjunction with them to push the animal upward toward the unsuspecting intruder.

Overhandling of any herptiles can be a source of trauma or shock to them. Depending on the individual, the shock can severely interrupt the feeding reaction. Kevin Bowler relates this instance concerning a seven-foot-long mugger crocodile which along with all of the other crocodilians had to be moved to temporary quarters during the building of Philadelphia's new reptile house. The moving job was of such scope that Ross Allen was called in to help and advise.

The mugger crocodile was big enough so that it had to be noosed and tied before being transported to the temporary quarters. Apparently the shock of such handling combined with the lack of amenities in temporary quarters caused it to go off feed for two years! It survived this fast only because it had been in top

Photo by the author

*Juvenile American crocodile.*

Photo by the a┆

*A pair of mugger crocod┆
Crocodylus palustris, baskin┆
a sandy bank. India, Pakistan┆
Sri Lanka (Ceylon) comprise┆
range of these large rept┆
where they are sometimes ┆
shipped by the Hindus.*

condition before with sufficient body weight to sustain it. The new reptile house was finished in a year and a half, so six months of the fast took place in its new environment. Fortunately, the new simulated natural habitat was more conducive to the mugger's temperament and it finally did resume feeding.

Compared to some crocodiles, the gavial, *Gavialis gangeticus* is not an aggressive crocodilian. The extremely narrow snout, which is its sure mark of identification, is especially adapted for catching fish—its main diet—underwater. The narrowness of the snout allows greater facility for fast slashes to the side to snag fish on the move, a feat the wider-snouted alligators and crocodiles have difficulty in accomplishing.

Apart from these differences, the crocodilians share a number of similarities which are uniquely adapted to their aquatic nature. They all have transparent third eyelids located at the front corner of the eyes which cover them for protection when swimming underwater, but allows the crocodilian limited vision to see where it is going. This third eyelid is known as a nictitating membrane. The ear openings and nostrils function somewhat like valves which the crocodilian can close when submerging underwater. The back of the large flat tongue also acts as a valve in the throat and allows the crocodilians to feed underwater without taking water into the lungs.

A close look at the skull structure of the crocodilians reveals the fact that they can move through the water with the important sensory organs (the eyes, nostrils and ears) above the surface of the water while the rest of the body is completely submerged. These senses are all well developed and very efficient and give the crocodilians the advantage of being better able to conceal their bulky bodies.

Their teeth are shed periodically as the functional set becomes less sharp or in the event that an individual tooth is lost or broken. Thus, the crocodilians always possess a sharp new set of teeth with which to grab their prey, "bear trap" style. It has been estimated that the closing pressure of an adult crocodilian's jaws

Photo by Andrew Koukoulis
gavial, Gavialis gangeticus, its long, slender snout to ure fish, which is one of its food items.

is about 1000 pounds—by comparison, the opening strength is weak.

Aside from strong jaws and sharp teeth, crocodilians also use their tails as a means of defense by slapping it at enemies or predators. All of the crocodilians possess a heavily-keeled tail which, when undulated back and forth, provides sure and powerful locomotion in the water. The front legs are folded against the sides of the body whereas the hind feet are used to stabilize the animal like twin rudders; they also help directional control while swimming on the bottom.

## VOICE

All crocodilians have a powerful and well-developed voice. The bellows and roars of an adult alligator must be equal in volume to that of a lion. It has been theorized that in the wild the males establish their territories by broadcasting their presence vocally. Here at the zoo I have heard our American alligators respond to the rumble of a passing truck with roars that seem to shake the building. Voice also serves the baby alligator well. When hatch-

Photo by Manuel *

*Crocodilians can move thro the water with their impor sensory organs (eyes, ears nostrils) above the surface o; water, while the rest of their remains almost completely merged.*

Photo by Zigmund Leszczynski

*An American alligator in its natural habitat.*

Photo by Saul Friess
*The author holding a yearling American alligator. Young gators grow about one foot a year until they reach 6 feet, then the rate of growth slows down.*

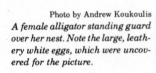

Photo by Andrew Koukoulis
*A female alligator standing guard over her nest. Note the large, leathery white eggs, which were uncovered for the picture.*

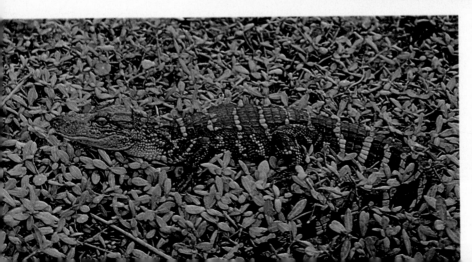

Photo by Saul Friess
*Hatchling alligators are brightly marked with yellow or orange bands running across the body and tail. They usually measure about 12 inches long when they emerge from the egg.*

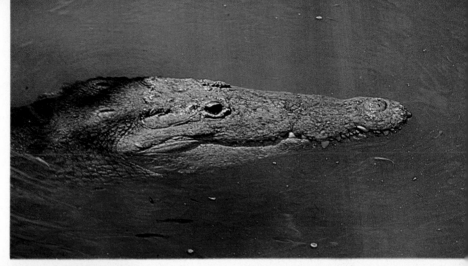

Photo by Saul Friess
*The American crocodile,* Crocodylus acutus, *is easily distinguished from the alligator by its narrow snout and the enlarged fourth tooth on the lower jaw which can be seen on the outside edges of the upper jaw.*

Photo by the author
*Young crocodiles are usually olive-brown with black markings and a yellowish belly; with age the color gradually changes to a dull gray.*

Photo by the author
*Close-up of an American crocodile. The ear opening behind the greenish-colored eye is quite distinct. A muscular flap of skin covers the ears and a fleshy valve covers the nostrils when a crocodilian submerges.*

Photo by Saul Friess
*Typicial habitat of the American alligator in southern South Carolina near the Savannah Wildlife Refuge.*

Photo by Saul Friess
*An adult gator floats quietly along the surface of a canal in the Florida Everglades.*

Photo by the author
*A crowded pool of alligators. Gators are exploited at roadside alligator "farms" throughout the southern United States.*

*s large bull gator,* Alligator *sissippiensis, would hiss and r whenever the zoo keeper red its enclosure. In the wild ? alligators establish their :tory by periodically bellow- with their powerful voice.*

ing, it emits high-pitched gruntlike sounds that stimulate the mother to help uncover the mound nest she has been guarding during the incubation of the eggs. Some scientists feel that many babies would die without that "cry for help," as the hatchlings are not strong enough to break through the crust of mud and decaying vegetation that forms the nest.

## RECUPERATIVE ABILITIES

The ability of the crocodilians to resist infection deserves special attention because it is unusual. One of my friends, Peter Brazaitis, cared for a gavial which had its entire lower jaw broken off in an accident when it was a juvenile. Miraculously the wound healed.

It had to be hand-fed with fish and meat and had learned to seize and swallow its food in spite of the handicap. The gavial grew to maturity and was normal in most other respects.

Photo by Andrew Kouk

*This stump-tailed gator demonstrates the hardiness of crocodilians. Although this specimen had some difficulty swimming it was normal in all other respects.*

Crocodilians have a superior infection-fighting blood characteristic. Research has shown that the number of white blood cells that gather around the site of any open wound is extraordinarily high. Healing of flesh wounds is almost inevitable. Of course, this does not include damage to a vital organ. In many cases crocodilians in the wild often have toes and pieces of tail missing as well as extensive scarification of the hide. However, they cannot regenerate their tails, as most lizards can.

## OUR VANISHING CROCODILIANS

In the United States, the American alligator and American crocodile are protected animals. After being overhunted for years because their hides were much in demand, the crocodilians can be classified among the vanishing animals of the world. This is the main reason why I discourage keeping any of the crocodilians as pets. We need to maintain the populations which we have and to reduce the profit motive in their capture to promote their survival.

Poaching and the pet trade constitute the biggest threat to the crocodilian populations of the world. The destruction of habitat has also greatly added to their disappearance. It has been estimated that despite the risks because it is illegal, dealing in crocodilian hides is a multi-million dollar business. Although the United States is a conservation leader in this matter, the laws are difficult to enforce in some states where a small number of park rangers are expected to patrol thousands of acres. Even the administration of fines defeats the naturalist; the maximum fine is only $1,000 and this is not enough to discourage professional poachers. The only sure way to stop poaching is to eliminate the market for crocodilian hides and pet store sales. Some states, such as New York, have already taken action to eliminate the sale of crocodilian hides completely.

Poachers hunt alligators at night with strong flashlights. The gators are easier to see at this time as their eyes glow a luminescent red-orange in the glare of the lights. The poacher then rows over and strikes the gator with an axe or sledgehammer in the area between the eyes. This blow to the brain kills the gator or renders it helpless. No firearms are used, as silence must mask the poacher's activities. Although the alligator is dead at this point, nerve impulses may cause the body to twitch for several hours. In order to stop these movements, the poacher will often take a piece of wire and push it down the alligator's spinal column until it reaches the tail. This disables the spinal cord and prevents any further movement. At that point the gator is skinned and the carcass thrown overboard.

Probably the saddest aspect of gator poaching is the small amount of hide that is actually used. In a manner reminiscent of the white man's slaughter of the bison for its tongue and hide only, the most prized and useful part of the alligator's skin is the underside. Many times the rest is discarded because processing it for use is so much more costly and time consuming.

The Nile crocodile, *Crocodylus niloticus,* has also become endangered by the intrusion of boat traffic on the parts of the rivers which have traditionally been egg-laying sites for the females. Typically, the female buries her eggs in the sandbanks of the river and stays to guard them until they are ready to hatch. Movement by the boats and human habitation on the rivers have frightened them away and the clutches of eggs are left to the Nile monitor lizards and other predators who dig them up and eat them.

In the United States the destruction and rechanneling of natural waterways has dried up many of the marshy habitats that once were the haunts of the American alligator. Of course, the ecology movement has had some impact and the American alligator populations are actually increasing in the wild, but a greater awareness on the part of the general public must be reached so that definite moves can be made to preserve the crocodilians of the world.

# AMERICAN ALLIGATOR
### *(Alligator mississippiensis)*

### *Size and Body Structure*

The American alligator is a heavy-bodied crocodilian with a flat head and tapering, muscular tail. The snout is blunt and rounded, a characteristic which prevents it from being confused with our only other native crocodilian, the American crocodile. The alligator's back is covered with several rows of horny scales which continue onto the tail, forming a keel. Under each one of these scales lies a bony plate. The belly scales do not have these underlying bony plates, and as a result of this, it is this part of the skin that is used in making leather. The legs of the alligator are short and rather weak. They are used mainly to aid the animal in crawling along the ground although it can raise itself up on its legs and run for short distances. In size alligators average from eight to ten feet in length, although specimens as long as fifteen feet have been found. The largest specimen ever recorded was nineteen feet two inches long. (Conant 1975)

### *Coloration*

Alligators are basically black with a yellowish-white belly, although specimens which have been out of the water for some time will appear to be dull gray. Young alligators have bright yellow or orange bands running across the body and tail. These bands fade with age and have usually disappeared by the time the animal attains a length of seven to eight feet.

### *Range*

The range of the alligator extends from southeastern North Carolina south to the Florida Keys and as far west as eastern Texas. It is difficult to give an accurate range for the American alligator since it has been exterminated in many of the areas where it was once common.

### Breeding Habits

The mating season of the American alligator runs from early May through late June, depending on the weather and geography. The beginning of the mating season is signaled by the bellowing of the male alligator. At this time the male also exudes a powerful musk from its scent glands. Actual mating takes place in the water after a long and elaborate courtship. The female is fertilized by internal penetration by the male. After a short gestation period, the female looks for a dry, sunny spot near the territory in the swamp where she has been living throughout the year.

Alligators do not bury their eggs in sandy soil on pond or river banks as turtles do, but instead build mound nests. The female gator scoops up mud and soil with her broad jaws and piles it up two or three feet high. Sticks, branches and other types of vegetation are often mixed into the mound. This material is important because as it rots it acts as a heat-generating medium and also allows for some air circulation. Once the construction is finished, the female lays some twenty or seventy eggs in two or three layers in a hollow at the top of the mound. The female then covers the top with more mud and sticks and packs it down by crawling over it.

Illustration by Florence Gibson

*erican alligators feed on a iety of small animals includ- fish, frogs and turtles as well birds and small mammals. tured here is a young gator turing a small bullfrog.*

The mound acts as an incubator for as the sun warms it during the day, it retains the heat at night. In addition, the temperature is also raised slightly by the rotting vegetation.

The incubation period is about eight or nine weeks. The female gator stands guard over her nest during this time and will attack

any intruder that threatens it. There are reports of female gators actually rushing at a man to scare him off when he ventures too close to her nest. After the incubation period is over, the baby gators cut through the eggshell with the aid of an "egg tooth." Once they begin to hatch, the cries of the hatchlings are heard by the female and she helps them break out of the mound. The baby gators move to the water and may remain with her for a period of time before the female returns to her regular tempo of life in the swamp.

## General Discussion

The first time I saw an alligator in the wild was back in April of 1964. Jim Bockowski and I were looking for scarlet kingsnakes *(Lampropeltis triangulum elapsoides)* by a roadside pond in South Carolina. We were busy ripping bark off of old stumps, and were completely unaware of a perfectly camouflaged four-foot-long American alligator right beside Jimmy. We saw it only when it gave a wild thrash of the tail as it dove to the deepest part of the pond.

One of my greatest pleasures has been in observing alligators in their natural habitat. I have watched them basking in the sun

Photo by Manuel

*An alligator basking on the of a canal in the Savan National Wildlife Refuge southern South Carolina. the large, muscular tail.*

on the dikes of the Savannah Wildlife Refuge near Savannah, Georgia. At the approach of a human they slip into the "alligator grass" at the water's edge. This matting of aquatic vegetation also provides good hiding places for the young gators, too.

On one trip it was my privilege to make the acquaintance of Bill Greene of Hardeeville, South Carolina. Having been born and raised in the area, he knows the country well and kindly consented to show me some of the streams and rivulets where I could observe alligators in their natural habitat.

One young gator had established itself under a small bridge over a dirt road. Mr. Greene took me to visit the bridge and sure enough we found the gator. It was three feet long and possessed the characteristic yellow markings; it was basking with the bottom of its feet turned toward the sun. I crept to within seven or eight feet of the gator, at which point it charged into the water to escape.

On another trip Mr. Greene introduced me to a large gator which had become so used to visiting tourists that it had lost its fear of man. Although it was eleven feet long, it was obvious that about one foot of its tail had been lost at an earlier point in life. We got close enough to take some very good photographs. Afterwards we were worried that it might be seen from the road, so I had to prod it with a stick to get it to move into the protection of the water.

One week later when we returned to the large lake which it shared with many other alligators, we found its lack of fear was almost its undoing. Poachers had attempted to capture or kill it, severely wounding the gator with an axe. Park Rangers caught them in the act and brought charges against them and the gator was moved to a safer and less frequented area where it was hoped its wounds would heal.

In addition to observing alligators in the wild, I have also worked with them in captivity as a reptile keeper. Once or twice a week I had to jump down among the ten American alligators in the pool to clean up the litter thrown among them by careless visitors. My only safety precaution was to take a broom or long pole as a prod to herd the alligators to one end of the enclosure in order to allow cleaning. Young children were especially fearful when they saw me down in the pool. Luckily, I could reassure them that alligators are not aggressive, especially when they are out of water and are used to being in close contact with man.

In fact, in the fall when our alligators must be brought indoors, these inoffensive reptiles provide an afternoon of entertainment for zoo visitors as all the keepers take part in our gator roundup.

Looking more like a corps of janitors than zoo keepers, we all enter the cage armed with brooms, poles and ropes. Each gator has to be noosed just behind the front legs and pulled forcibly to the inside pool. Everyone gets wet, including the spectators. We worry most about hitting our heads on the low clearance doors, not from any attack from the gators. This would not be so were we dealing with some kinds of crocodiles; they are far more aggressive!

During the winter months the alligators at the Staten Island Zoo are kept cool and they go off feed. In early May, as the temperature rises, they seem to sense the approach of warmer weather and become much more active. When herded outside for the summer their appetites take a decided upturn, as do all facets of their behavior. They hiss at us and gape their mouths in warning. On several occasions we have even been snapped at by a big bull alligator that is approximately eleven and a half feet long. A little fast "broom work" is then necessary to ward it off.

During my first months as a zoo keeper we housed sixteen American alligators ranging in size from three feet to eleven and a half feet. Feeding time takes place at 4:00 P.M. for the edification

Photo by Andrew Kouk

*A gator eating a fish, a common item on their food list.*

of zoo visitors. The alligators were fed seventy-five to eighty pounds of horsemeat chunks and seventy-five to 100 pounds of fish. The latter consisted mostly of whiting with some bluefish, snappers and porgies added. In order to ensure proper distribution of the food, it is hand-fed to the gators. That is to say we hold the food out to the various alligators on long forceps.

As soon as the food pan appears, the entire group comes thrashing to the edge of the pool. Some of the larger ones even manage to get their heads up over the edge of the retaining wall, a rather unnerving sight, to say the least.

One Sunday in the summer of 1965, we were performing our weekly ritual when a very eager and agile 175 pounds of gator not only took the meat that I was offering, but also got a firm hold on the forceps that I was using. Because the handle of these forceps were of the scissors type, I was sure that my fingers would be wrenched from my hand. However, that problem did not stay foremost in mind because the gator was slowly pulling me into the pool. At that point I was scared! Luckily I grabbed the guard rail which prevented me from being pulled in. With all my strength, and thanks to what must have been large amounts of adrenalin pouring into my system, I pulled the alligator up from the water and then quickly dropped it, giving me the momentary slack which I needed to slip my thumb and fingers from the forceps. The gator swallowed the meat—forceps and all!

The next day, while my hand was still aching from the strain, I found the regurgitated forceps along with many broken teeth at the bottom of the pool. This was physical evidence of the orgy of feeding time. I feel sure that had I fallen into the water I would have been attacked as a food source, as surely as a chunk or horse meat or fish.

Alligators are both interesting and important animals. Their integration into the wildlife community is not only that of a controller of animal populations by feeding on mammals, birds, turtles, etc., but it also includes that of preserver. Alligators build winter quarters by burrowing into pond or river banks. The excavated soil is mounded along the bank, giving anchorage for trees and shrubs that in turn provide nesting for birds and food for deer. Gator holes are somewhat similar to the beaver dam in the benefits to be derived from them, the holes also serve as watering places when the drought season comes and the shallower waterways dry up. Some aquatic species of animals would perish if it were not for these gator-engineered reservoirs. For that contribution of the alligator to the ecology and survival of other species, we should be grateful.

# AMERICAN CROCODILE
*(Crocodylus acutus)*

### *Size and Body Structure*

The American crocodile is very similar in appearance to the American alligator. In fact, the physical description given for the alligator could very well fit the American crocodile, with two important exceptions. One is that the crocodile possesses a narrow, tapering snout, whereas the alligator has a broad, rounded one. The other difference involves the teeth. In the American crocodile, the fourth tooth on each side of the lower jaw protrudes outside of the mouth and is quite visible when the mouth is closed. In the American alligator this tooth fits into a socket in the upper jaw. The American crocodile grows to an average length of seven and a half to twelve feet with the record-size specimen being twenty-three feet long.

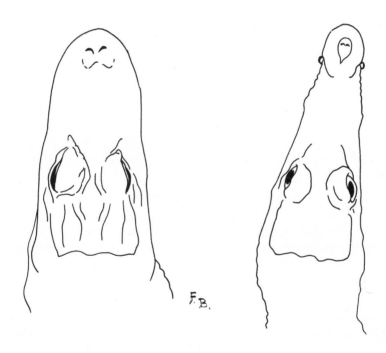

*American alligator, left*
*American crocodile, right*

### *Coloration*

American crocodiles are generally olive-brown with a yellowish belly. In old specimens, those over ten feet long, the color changes to a dull gray. Young individuals are greenish-brown with black spots.

### Range

In the United States, the American crocodile is now found only in extreme southern Florida and on and near the Keys. It also occurs in the West Indies, southern Mexico and the coastal areas of Ecuador, Colombia, and Venezuela.

### Breeding Habits

Photo by Andrew Koukoulis

*American crocodile basking; palms of the feet are turned ward, to dehydrate any ex- nal parasites that may be esent.*

Our knowledge of the breeding habits of the American crocodile is rather limited, especially in the areas of courtship and mating behavior. As a result of a National Park Service study undertaken by John C. Ogden, a staff biologist, and Caulion Singletary, a photographer, at a breeding site in Florida Bay, however, some information about nesting activity is known. Unlike the American alligator, the female American crocodile builds her nest out of

sand. The nest is usually about two feet high and ten feet across, and the eggs are buried about ten inches below the surface. The incubation period lasts for approximately three and one-half months. Near the end of the period, the female visits the nest every night. During these visits the female rests her head across the center of the mound so that she will be able to either feel or hear the young as they are hatching. When she senses that the young crocodiles are hatching, the female will dig them out of the nest, gently pick them up in her jaws and release them at the water's edge. She will repeat this procedure until all of the baby crocodiles are in the water (Odgen 1973). At this time the hatchlings are only nine inches long, but if they are able to escape the constant threat of predators they may someday grow to a length of over fourteen feet.

### General Discussion

Scientists were unaware of the presence of the American crocodile in Florida until 1875 when the naturalist William T. Hornaday discovered a fourteen-foot specimen in Biscayne Bay. At that time, American crocodiles were fairly common in most of the coastal lands below Lake Okeechobee. Now, due to the predation of man, it is on the verge of extinction in the United States. Great efforts are being made by the Everglades National Park Rangers to save the American crocodile. Staff biologist John Ogden, also responsible for the nesting activity study cited earlier tells me that the estimated population of the American crocodile in the Everglades and Florida Keys is only somewhere between 300 to 600 individuals. That is not a bad population level as long as poachers let them alone and give them a chance to breed in their natural habitat. These crocodiles are the last of the species found naturally in the United States. It would be a sad blow to the conservation of our wildlife if the American crocodile should become extinct in this country.

# SPECTACLED CAIMAN
### (Caiman crocodilus)
### (Introduced into southern Florida)

### Size and Body Structure

In its general shape and body structure the young caiman closely resembles other young crocodilians, but the spectacled caiman

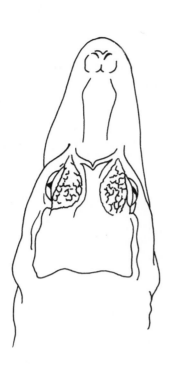
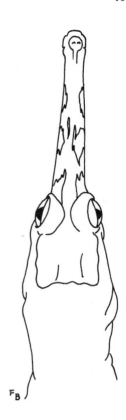

*spectacled caiman, near right*
*gavail, far right*

possesses a curved ridge of bone running from the corner of one eye to the other. This ridge makes the caiman appear to be wearing a pair of eyeglasses, thus giving rise to the common name of spectacled caiman. Should you come across a baby crocodilian being offered for sale, you should report any such illegal sale effort to the United States Fish and Wildlife Service immediately.

Although the caimans offered for sale in pet shops are usually about ten to twelve inches long, they can grow quite large. The record size for the spectacled caiman is eight feet, eight inches. (Conant 1975)

### Coloration

The caiman is beige to light brown with several dark brown to black crossbars on the body and tail.

### Range

The spectacled caiman is found in marshes and streams from southern Mexico to central South America and has been introduced into the Everglades of southern Florida and possibly into other southern states with warm climates.

### General Discussion

Baby caimans prefer a temperature range between 80° F. and 85° F. This is the most critical factor for proper body function and growth. In the wild the hatchling caiman begins its carnivorous existence by feeding on insects, small frogs, and fishes. These make up the bulk of its diet for the first year of its life. Movement of the prey animals stimulates the feeding reaction.

The rapid growth characteristics of young crocodilians is, I am sure, a survival mechanism that protected the many species until their encounter with man. They almost double their size in the first year. As the caiman gets larger, fish, frogs, mammals, birds, and other reptiles are consumed. Under ideal conditions, at the zoo we have annual growth records of over a foot for each specimen. The crocodilian is a complete carnivore. It will eat any

Photo by the aut

*The spectacled caiman, once popular animal in the pet tra is now considered an endange species. It has been introduc into the Florida Everglad where this individual u captured.*

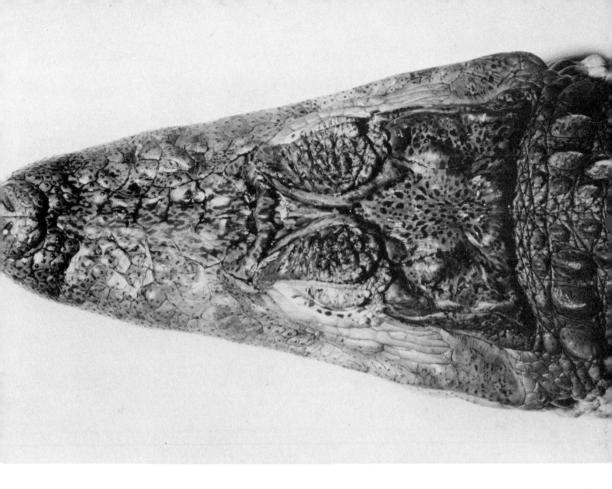

Photo by the author

*chief identifying character-*
*cs of the spectacled caiman,*
*man crocodilus, is the curved*
*ge of bone between the eyes.*

animal once it has grown enough to capture such prey. Documented cases of man-eating crocodiles are known from tropical countries where crocodiles occur. It must be remembered, however, that crocodiles do not hunt solely for human beings to eat. From the crocodile's point of view, a person bending down at the edge of a pond or stream to collect water probably looks much like an antelope or other animal that would form a normal part of its diet. This is probably how many cases of crocodile attacks on man can be accounted for. Man certainly does not form an important part of any crocodilian's diet.

It has been estimated that given 5 pounds of fish or meat, the crocodilian successfully converts 2¼ to 2½ pounds of that food to its own body weight, which is a tremendously efficient rate of conversion. A crocodilian does not use much energy in movement, and it spends long periods of time absolutely motionless, much to the frustration of many zoo visitors. This habit helps them in the wild though. When lying motionless on a muddy river bank, they look like a log or mud bar, and prospective prey may approach them unsuspectingly.

Photo by Saul Fries

*The American alligator wa*
*placed on the endangered specie*
*list of the United States Depart*
*ment of the Interior in 1968, an*
*is protected by federal law. If lef*
*undisturbed in its natural habita*
*the alligator will prosper, an*
*may eventually reoccupy habitat*
*where it has long been extermi*
*nated.*

One of the reasons for the crocodilian's long periods of stillness is its need to bask in the sun. In nature this is its way of obtaining the vitamin D needed to maintain proper calcium and phosphorus balance in the body. In captivity, this is not necessary as they can be provided with these vitamin requirements artificailly.

# AN ACCOUNT OF WORLD SPECIES

The following is a list of the 21 species of crocodilians known to occur in the world today. This classification was originally according to Wermuth and Mertens (1961).

## CROCODILIANS OF THE WORLD

| Species and Current Status | Distribution | Habitat | Maximum Length |
|---|---|---|---|
| American Alligator** *Alligator mississippiensis* | Coastal from North Carolina to east Texas and south Arkansas | Swamps, marshes, rivers, lakes, ponds | 19 ft. 2 in. |
| Chinese Alligator** *Alligator sinensis* | Lower Yangtze River Basin, China | Ponds, alluvial flood plains | 6 ft. |
| Spectacled Caiman** *Caiman crocodilus* | South Mexico to central South America | Swamps, marshes, rivers, streams | 8 ft. 8 in. |
| Broad-snouted Caiman** *Caiman latirostris* | Eastern and central South America | Small rivers, streams, lakes, ponds, marshes, along rivers | 7 ft. |
| Black Caiman** *Melanosuchus niger* | Amazon River Basin, South America | Swamps, marshy streams, small lakes, ponds | 15 ft. |
| Dwarf Caiman* *Paleosuchus palpebrosus* | North and central South America | Shaded bodies of still water in tropical rain forest | 5 ft. |
| Smooth-fronted Caiman* *Paleosuchus trigonatus* | North and central South America | Shaded bodies of moving waters in tropical rain forest | 7 ft. |
| American Crocodile** *Crocodylus acutus* | South Florida to Venezuela and Ecuador | Coastal regions, rivers, lakes | 23 ft. |
| African Slender-snouted Crocodile*** *Crocodylus cataphractus* | West and central Africa | Rivers, streams in forested areas | 8 ft. |
| Orinoco Crocodile *Crocodylus intermedius* | Orinoco River Basin South America | Large rivers and their tributaries | 23 ft. |
| Johnson's Crocodile** *Crocodylus johnsoni* | North Australia | Freshwater lagoons, billabongs, rivers | 8 ft. |
| Morelet's Crocodile** *Crocodylus moreleti* | South Mexico to British Honduras and northeast Guatemala | Freshwater swamps, slow moving rivers, streams | 8 ft. |

| Species and Current Status | Distribution | Habitat | Maximum Length |
|---|---|---|---|
| Nile Crocodile** *Crocodylus niloticus* | Africa, south of the Sahara, Madagascar | Rivers, lakes, swamps, some coastal situations | 18 ft. |
| New Guinea Crocodile** *Crocodylus novaeguineae* | New Guinea and certain islands in the Philippines | Freshwater marshes, ponds near rivers, lakes | 9 ft. 6 in. |
| Mugger Crocodile** *Crocodylus palustris* | India, Pakistan, Bangladesh, Ceylon | Rivers, ponds, swamps, brackish lagoons | 13 ft. |
| Saltwater Crocodile* *Crocodylus porosus* | South Ceylon, Indonesia, Philippines, to north Australia | Coastal marshes, estuaries, rivers, lakes | 20 ft. |
| Cuban Crocodile*** *Crocodylus rhombifer* | Zapata Swamp, Cuba | Freshwater swamps, marshes, known from coast in one area | 12 ft. |
| Siamese Crocodile** *Crocodylus siamensis* | Southeast Asia, Java | Freshwater swamps, slow moving streams, rivers | 11 ft. 6 in. |
| African Dwarf Crocodile** *Osteolaemus tetraspis* | West and central Africa | Quiet waters of rivers, streams in forested areas | 6 ft. |
| False Gavial** *Tomistoma schlegeli* | South Malay Peninsula, Sumatra, Borneo | Quiet waters of rivers, lakes | 16 ft. |
| Gavial*** *Gavialis gangeticus* | North India, Pakistan, Bangladesh, Burma | Large rivers | 21 ft. 6 in. |

KEY:       *     Declining
          **    Endangered
          ***   Critically endangered


## DON'T KEEP CROCODILIANS AS PETS!

Most species of crocodilians are protected by law. This means that these animals cannot be captured, kept, exported or sold legally to private individuals. As a result, the unfortunate species that has taken the place of the American alligator in the pet trade is the spectacled caiman. Once an animal found in great abundance, this crocodilian is seriously threatened regardless of the laws that are supposed to protect it in parts of its natural habitat. To help it and all other species, no crocodilian should be kept as a pet.

One can only hope that world opinion and the influence of conservation organizations will soon have more effect. Professional research helps us to understand these endangnered reptiles and provides us with the information necessary to help them. Observing or photographing these animals in the wild or in zoos instead of trying to keep them in captivity is the best contribution you can make.

A secondary word of discouragement is, admittedly, my own personal opinion—crocodilians do *not* make good pets. Although they are easy to handle when small, they can grow a foot a year under ideal conditions. Assuming that the keeper of any pet animal is able to provide proper conditions, you can see that within five years its owner would have a five or six-foot crocodilian on his or her hands. How many amateurs are equipped or prepared for that eventuality? Most of the crocodilians brought into the zoo are stunted in size or otherwise deformed in some way. This is due to improper diet and poor living quarters and conditions.

Most crocodilians do *not* have good dispositions. They become more irritable as they grow, and security precautions become an important factor. At the Staten Island Zoo the keepers still hear hisses of warning from the bull alligators when they use the catwalks above the alligator pool, even though the gators have been in captivity for many years!

I hope that the above information will discourage you from wanting to keep *any* crocodilian as a pet.

# Part II
# TURTLES

# Chapter 3

# INTRODUCTION TO TURTLES

Of the five reptilian orders known to exist in the world today, the turtles (order Chelonia) are by far the most popular and best accepted by mankind. People usually find turtles attractive in one way or another. Some persons think they possess a great charm; others may say they have sad, lonely faces. Turtles have "character" and lots of it. Whatever one wishes to interpret when looking at a turtle, it is there to see, etched by the millions of years they have survived as a group. The unique structure of their shells has long been a source of interest. Biologists are still studying the unknown habits of a few secretive or rare species.

Many human families have had a pet turtle at one time or another. Even though turtles have become familiar animals to most people, many uninformed turtle fanciers fail to realize that turtles are actually reptiles and are closely related to such creatures as crocodiles and snakes.

## WHAT IS A TURTLE?

A turtle, by definition, is a reptile with a bony or leathery shell. Most, but not all, have medium to large-sized heads. Teeth are lacking; instead, the jaws are provided with a sharp, horny, beaklike cutting edge. Turtles characteristically have four strong, clawed or flipperlike limbs and a tail. Some are terrestrial and such turtles often have highly domelike shells and elephantlike feet. Others are semiaquatic and have pronounced webbing between their toes, whereas still others are totally aquatic (marine), and have modified limbs that are paddlelike in shape. All turtles reproduced by internal fertilization and lay eggs on land.

## USEFULNESS AND RELATIONSHIP TO MAN

Turtles were on this planet for a very long time before man appeared. Their ancestors no doubt "watched" as our own ancestors plodded their way upward through the centuries. Slowly, over hundreds of thousands of years, we progressed and developed until we became the dominant creatures on earth. Man did not need great strength or extraordinary speed, nor did he need sharp claws or long fangs to survive. He had something that proved to be far more lethal than any of these. Man had a brain with which to think and figure out his problems and he eventually outsmarted other animals that shared the environment with him. Man thought of the wheel and the lever, the knife and

Photo by the au*
*The author's son Robert meets*
*adult female Yellow Bell*
*Turtle,* Chrysemys *scri*
scripta.

and spear, the cotton gin and the telephone; he learned to split peas for soup, then the atom for war. Today man is by far the worst predator of all; he kills and destroys in the name of progress or for sport. The result has been mass destruction of natural areas and the doom of many animal species. Even at the time of this writing, when ecology, pollution and conservation are household words, there are many rare plants and animals that are still being threatened with extinction. With all our technical knowledge and accomplishments, we have not learned to share the environment with other creatures and plants that live on this planet with us. There is indeed much cause for dismay as we contemplate our vanishing wilderness and wildlife.

Words like "slow" and "lazy" are often used to describe turtles, yet neither of these accurately describes a turtle's personality. A more appropriate word would be "conservative." Back in prehistoric times, chelonians learned to be conservative reptiles, and they are basically the same creatures now as they were then. They have managed far better than we human beings in the game of survival. Turtles watched the dinosaurs come and go; they saw many kinds of mammals evolve and vanish; and finally, they watched man assume dominance.

The ancient Roman soldiers may have fashioned one of their battle formations with the shell of a turtle in mind, for that strategy was called the Turtle (Testudo). During battle the soldiers marched across the field in an oval formation with their shields held overhead forming a "carapace," while the men on the outside perimeter held their shields to their sides. Thus they formed what looked like a giant turtle advancing toward the enemy. Such a formation offered the Roman soldiers almost full protection from enemy arrows and spears dispatched in their direction.

Throughout history many cultures all around the world have considered turtles as objects of reverence. Many treated them as sacred, or conferred upon them high religious significance. Turtles also found their way into our American folklore and children's stories. Everyone has heard the famous Greek fable about the race between the tortoise and the hare. Many modifications have been made on the basic story; even Warner Brothers' famous cartoon character Bugs Bunny once raced with a turtle.

The turtles' role as a food source has probably constituted their main relationship with man. Since long before the dawn of history, many species of turtles have been eaten by various peoples. During the 19th century, sailors from whaling vessels stopped at the Galápagos Islands off the cost of Ecuador to procure tortoises

Photo by Marty Mar
courtesy of the Philadelphia

*A herd of gaint galapagos t
toises,* Geochelone elephantop
*at the Philadelphia Zoo. Here
large male attempts to moun
smaller-sized female. Few z
have been successful in their
deavor to breed this endange
species.*

for meat. Proof of this can still be seen on some of the islands; the names of sailors and their vessels were carved in the rocks long ago. Giant tortoises were collected by the scores or even hundreds and placed aboard the ships. They provided the crew with fresh meat for a period of six months or more. The tortoises usually remained alive that long without food and could be killed as they were needed. The giant tortoises used as a source of fresh meat and oil by sailors and Ecuadorian natives belong to the family Testudinidae and the genus *Geochelone.*

It is probable that no other group of trutles has suffered more from man's predatory habits than the sea turtles of the family Cheloniidae. Of these, the green turtle, *Chelonia mydas,* is the species most sought because of its delicious meat. The name "green" turtle comes not from the color of the shell, which is usually brownish, olive, or bluish-black, but from the color of its fat.

In the United States two turtles have been in demand as food for man: the diamondback terrapin, *Malaclemys terrapin,* and the snapping turtle, *Chelydra serpentina.* Both species are col- lected and trapped throughout their range by amateur and pro-

Photo by Saul Friess

Photo by Saul Friess

*The Green Sea Turtle,* Chelonia mydas, *the northern diamond-back terrapin,* Malaclemys terrapin terrapin, *and the snapping turtle,* Chelydra serpentina serpentina, *are three species of North American turtle frequently eaten by man.*

Photo by the author

fessional turtle hunters. The snapping turtle's popularity as a food item reaches its peak in the Philadelphia area. In that city many restaurants feature snapper soup or stew on their menus.

At the Fulton Fish Market in New York City several fish companies offer both snapping turtles and terrapins for sale during certain months. However, the terrapins were sold far more frequently than the snappers. Some large sea turtles are also occasionally sold. I once saw a fish dealer with cases of live diamondback terrapins; each case contained several dozen individuals piled on top of one another, and sprinkled with ice. One box had three large snapping turtles crammed in it; these were about twenty-five pounds each and still in good condition in spite of the crowded quarters. Terrapin stew was a popular dish back in the 1900s and up to the 30s. During that time the turtle populations in the northeastern states became very low because of over-collecting. With so many other foods available today, the Diamondback is too difficult for most people to prepare, and the species has made a fantastic comeback in recent years. Diamondback terrapins still occur in the coastal waters and tidal marshes of both Long Island and Staten Island, New York.


## ORIGIN AND EVOLUTION

The origin of turtles dates back some 250 million years to the Carboniferous period. Paleontologists have been able to link turtle ancestors to the "stem" reptiles (cotylosaurs) which were the basic reptilian stock from which all other reptiles arose. One of the basic characteristics of our present-day turtles is the anapsid skull, a skull with a solid cranium and no temporal openings. The fossil remains of the old cotylosaurs also have anapsid skulls, which suggests some relationship. To this day no paleontologist has found any transitional fossils with turtle characters, only fossils with some slight intermediate characters.

If one tried to trace turtle ancestry, he would not find a fossil that was clearly turtlelike until he examined fossils from the early Triassic period. This was some 185 million years ago. Fossil evidence links a small reptile called *Eunotosaurus africanus* to the modern-day turtles. This turtlelike creature existed in the Permian period in South Africa. Although teeth are present in its jaws, the eight wide ribs, which almost touch each other, suggest the formation of a turtle's upper shell. However, its fossil remains are poorly preserved and incomplete and do not give a clear picture of its exact anatomy, only a suggestion of intermediate characters.

The late Alfred Romer (1956, 1966), a famous paleontologist, suggested that "although *Eunotosaurus africanus* is not a true turtle, it is far from being a typical Cotylosaur."

Towards the end of the Triassic period there evolved another turtlelike reptile called *Triassochelys*. Similar to *Eunotosaurus africanus, Triassochelys* also had the anapsid skull with teeth. This indicates some possible relationship between these ancient creatures. It is believed that these primitive turtlelike reptiles were amphibious in habits and could eat in or out of water. The upper shell and the lower belly shields were fairly well developed, but it is unlikely that the head and limbs could be pulled into the shell at this period of the turtle's evolution.

Some of these turtlelike animals were largely terrestrial in habits, whereas other kinds returned to an aquatic existence. As time went on, the shell was modified to suit the particular habitat niche that the species occupied and to offer the greatest amount of protection. Other changes of anatomy were also taking place: by now the teeth were gone, replaced by a tough, horny covering on the beaklike jaws. Some of these reptiles evolved streamlined shells and powerful legs with pronounced webbing for swimming, while others developed thick, high-domed shells and elephantine feet for life on land. This diversity in habitat preference allowed turtles to survive on all fronts, so to speak. Other kinds of small reptiles were constantly falling prey to larger predators, while the turtles survived (in some cases, but not all) because of the protection of their shell.

Among one of the largest groups of turtles, the Cryptodira, there emerged a seagoing turtle called *Archelon*. It had many characteristics of some of the marine turtles of today, e.g., the leatherbacks, *Dermochelys coriacea:* a tough layer of thick, leathery skin with a mosaic of small separate bones covered their backs instead of the hard bony shell that other turtles developed. *Archelon* had well developed flipperlike feet for an aquatic life in Cretaceous seas, and grew to tremendous size, as fossil evidence has shown. One fossil specimen measured almost eleven feet in length and twelve feet in width at the front forefeet (Carr 1963). Other turtle fossils, dating back some 80 million years, were found in the famous Niobrara chalk beds of Kansas. One six-foot sea turtle called *Protostega* was found perfectly preserved by petrifaction.

Why turtles survived the mysterious and sudden misfortune of most reptilian orders during the end of the Mesozoic era remains one of the mysteries of science. It seems as though the turtles, as a group, found a good thing and stuck to it; for they have remained relatively unchanged for the past 150 million years, since the disaster of the Mesozoic era.

While other reptiles began to die off, one after another, the turtles learned one of nature's most important laws. That law was "adapt or perish," and they quickly made the necessary adjustments which helped them survive along with a few other reptilian orders. They adopted a more or less stereotyped physique in this constantly changing planet. This law is still quite accurate today and holds true for man himself: "Adapt or perish."

## ANATOMY

The carapace is composed of the vertebral column (backbone) and the rib cage. These have grown together with bony plates that start in the skin. The plastron protects the ventral parts of the turtle's body, and is also composed of bony shields and plates. These may or may not have a hinge, depending on the species in question. Another exceptional part of the turtle's anatomy is the position of the limb girdles, the bones that support the legs. These are located inside the rib cage. The shell bones partially embrace the shoulder and pelvic girdles, enabling the turtle's limbs to hang from a point within the bony ribs of the carapace.

These astonishing anatomical developments, which occurred long ago by the slow process of evolution, were one of the most important factors assisting the turtle's survival.

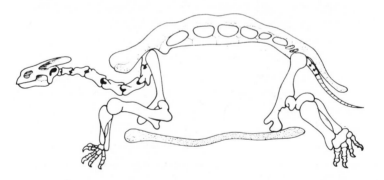

Illustration by Florence Bramley

*Skeleton of turtle*

## RESPIRATION

Since a turtle's ribs are part of the carapace, these bones are not able to help in expanding the chest for breathing as is the case with most mammals. Early herpetologists believed that the movements of a turtle's throat represented muscle impulses which pumped air into the larynx, similar to the breathing process of frogs and toads, but this was not so. It was later determined that three special muscles control the breathing functions of the lungs. Inhalation is accomplished by two flank muscles (one at each leg socket) beneath the viscera. The action of these muscles enlarges the body cavity so that air enters the lungs, somewhat similar to the way mammals utilize the diaphragm, the muscular partition separating the chest from the abdomen. Air is expelled by a complex ventral muscle which pushes the viscera against the lungs, thus forcing the air out. The movements of the throat are only secondary actions to the muscles that control the breathing, and may help with the turtle's keen olfactory senses.

## BODY STRUCTURE

Of all the vertebrate animals known to science, none has caused more speculation and controversy among scientists than the turtle. The reason for this is the unique anatomy of the shell which all turtles possess to some degree. What is a turtle's shell, and what is so unusual about it?

Most vertebrate animals, including man, have soft flesh that is covered with scales, feathers, hair, or just bare skin, and which, in turn, protects the bones of the skeletal structure. A turtle, in complete contrast, has most of its bones on the outside of its body, protecting the soft flesh and vital organs. An added advantage which most turtles have is the ability to withdraw head and limbs inside the armorlike shell for further protection against predators. A few species have on the lower shell a special hinge that closes tightly when the head and limbs are fully withdrawn. A classic example of a hinged turtle is the box turtle, *Terrapene carolina*. Its single belly-hinge allows it complete closure of the shell.

Children's storybooks and cartoons would have us believe that turtles can come out of their shells. This is not so; simply put, it is impossible for a turtle to leave its shell because its backbone and ribs are firmly attached to form the upper part of the shell. One would have to kill a turtle and perform a dissection in order to remove the body and limbs from the outside shell. Beneath the bony plates there lies a membrane called the parietal peritoneum, which forms an inner lining of the shell where it surrounds the vital organs.

A turtle's shell is divided into an upper part, which her-

Photo by Zigmund Leszczy

*The Eastern Box Turtle, T*
*rapene carolina carolina, i*
*classic example of a hinged tur*
*Its single belly-hing allows*
*complete withdrawal of its he*
*tail, and limbs into the protec*
*of the shell.*

petologists call a carapace, and a lower part, which is called a plastron. The carapace and plastron are connected on each side by lateral bridges which leave open the front and back portions between the upper and lower shells. This allows great freedom of movement for the limbs and tail; most important, the head can be completely withdrawn.

Most turtles possess other means of respiration to augment the action of the lungs. Some aquatic species use the lining of the mouth cavity as a sort of gill by bringing water in and out of the nasal openings. Dissolved oxygen is extracted from the water by the highly vascular pharyngeal passage (the pharynx), in the mouth and throat region. This secondary method of gathering oxygen greatly increases a turtle's ability to remain submerged in cold weather.

Some turtles possess still another means of aquatic respiration to supplement the action of the pharynx. This method of respiration is accomplished when a turtle takes water into the anal opening, where two thin-walled sacs are filled and emptied, causing a slow current. These vascular sacs, which communicate with the cloaca, serve as another oxygen gathering area. Most

Photo by Saul Friess

*A* northern diamondback terrapin, Malaclemys terrapin terrapin, *pushes out of its egg. Notice the horny skin modification on the snout called a caruncle. This projection aids the hatchling in cutting through the leathery shell.*

Photo by Zigmund Leszczynski
*The snapping turtle, Chelydra serpentina serpentina, is a large, ugly turtle that is easily recognized by its quick temper and willingness to defend itself with sharp scissorlike jaws.*

Photo by the author
*The snapping turtle is basically a rather drab turtle, but occasionally a brightly marked individual turns up, like the young adult pictured here with yellowish lines radiating from the center of each shield.*

Photo by the author
*A hatchling snapping turtle is usually about one inch long when it emerges from the egg. This specimen still has the caruncle visable on its snout.*

Photo by Saul Friess
*An adult female stinkpot basking on a log in the morning sun. Musk turtles are known for their climbing propensities.*

Photo by the author
*Stinkpots can easily be recognized by two prominent yellowish white lines on the side of the head. Notice the barbels on the chin of this adult male.*

Photo by Saul Friess
*Hatchling stinkpots emerge from the nest around the beginning of September, measuring about an inch in length. The carapace is heavily keeled and the face markings are distinct.*

*Mud turtles have a smooth carapace with no distinctive pattern or marks. The shell is usually a shade of brown and most have yellowish markings on the sides of the head, that occasionally form lines onto the neck.*

*This adult male mud turtle displays its strongly hooked jaws and mean disposition.*

*Quite frequently mud turtles can be found a great distance from water. In southern South Carolina it was a common occurence during the spring to find them in "stump-holes".*

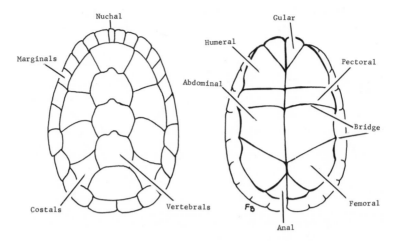

Illustrations by Florence Bramley

*Upper shell; the carapace*      *Lower shell; The plastron*

aquatic turtles possess the ability to withdraw oxygen from the water by using one or both of the above techniques. Soft-shelled turtles of the family Trionychidae are probably the most independent of all turtles on aquatic respiration, utilizing their skin as well as other methods.

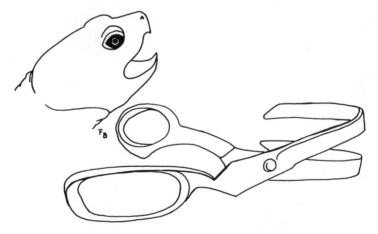

Illustration by Florence Bramley

*The curved scissors illustrate the shearing action of a turtle's jaws.*

## THE RETRACTABLE HEAD

One question often asked is: "How are turtles able to withdraw their heads inside their shells?" The answer to this question is rather difficult to understand unless one is familiar with the anatomy of a turtle. A turtle's neck is long and extremely flexible, thus enabling it to bend it at the most extraordinary angles. This is accomplished by a special arrangement of the neck vertebrae and the accompanying muscles. The skin that covers the neck is also highly flexible, and stretches along with the muscles when the turtle extends its head as far as it will go.

There are two basic methods by which turtles retract their heads into the shell. These are most important differences and form the basis by which all living members of the group are classified.

## CLASSIFICATION

Herpetologists place turtles in the order Testudines. Within this order there are about twelve families which include more than 200 species. These are well distributed around the world, occurring on all major continents with tropical or semitropical climates. In the case of marine turtles, they are most commonly found in tropical oceanic waters.

Because turtles have an anapsid skull, they have been placed in the subclass Anapsida, within which they constitute an order of shelled reptiles called Testudines. The order is then subdivided into two suborders, called Pleurodira and Cryptodira.

The Pleurodira are commonly known as the side-neck turtles. These turtles withdraw their heads by bending their necks to the side. For the most part, the side-neck turtles are highly aquatic, with the greatest concentrations occurring in Australia. They are also found in Africa, Madagascar, and South America. At one time the suborder Pleurodira also occurred in North America, as shown by fossil evidence, but for some unknown reason it disappeared during the Cretaceous period.

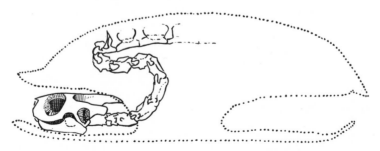

Illustration by Florence Gibson

*As this diagram clearly shows, a turtle's neck vertebrae are extremely flexible, thus enabling it to bend it in the most unusual ways, and allowing it to withdraw its head into the shell.*

The Cryptodira are the turtles with the "hidden necks." These are turtles that withdraw their heads by folding the neck into an S-shaped curve. This is a large and diverse suborder with representatives in Europe, Asia, Africa, and North and South America. They occur in Australia only as marine turtles; none are found on the land mass itself.

All of the known forms of turtles found in North America are Cryptodirans (hidden-necks). Seven families occur in the United States and adjacent tropical and temperate oceans:

1. Chelydridae, the snapping turtles
2. Kinosternidae, the mud and musk turtles
3. Emydidae, the aquatic, semiaquatic, and box turtles
4. Testudinidae, the desert and gopher tortoises
5. Cheloniidae, the aquatic sea turtles
6. Dermochelyidae, the leatherback sea turtle
7. Trionychidae, the softshell turtles

Of the seven families, the largest is Emydidae, with some twenty-five species distributed over the entire United States. Kinosternidae is basically a tropical American family, but some eight species range northward into this country. Cheloniidae, our marine turtles, have five species occurring in our warm coastal waters and around the Hawaiian Islands, whereas the family Dermochelyidae has but one species, the leatherback, *Dermochelys coriacea*. The latter two families form a super-family called Cheloniodae. The soft-shells of the family Trionychidae are a widespread group of turtles in this country. Three species are found within the continental United States, while a fourth (Asian) form has been introduced into the Hawaiian Island of Kavai. Chelydridae, the snapping turtle family, is strictly New World and contains two species: the monstrous alligator snapper, *Macroclemys temmincki,* and the wide-ranging common snapping turtle, *Chelydra serpentina*. The last family, Testudinidae, the totally terrestrial tortoises, is restricted to the southern United States. There are three species. In the pages which follow, each of these families will be discussed, some in great detail.

# Chapter 4

# SNAPPING TURTLES

Snapping turtles (Family Chelydridae) are a New World family with representatives in both North and South America. The family contains two genera: the common snapper, genus *Chelydra,* and the alligator snapper, genus *Macroclemys.*

There are two subspecies within the genus *Chelydra* in the United States—the common snapping turtle, *Chelydra serpentina serpentina,* and the Florida snapping turtle, *Chelydra serpentina osceola.* There are also two subspecies that are not found in this country. One occurs in Mexico, the other in South America to Ecuador.

The alligator snapping turtle, *Macroclemys temmincki,* is the sole member of its genus, and is restricted to the southeastern United States.

Of all freshwater species in North America, the snappers are the largest turtles. They are notorious for their aggressive nature and certainly live up to their common name. Members of this small family have large heads, strong sharp jaws, long tails, and powerful legs. The large carapace is sometimes rough, and the six marginals along the back edge of the shell are jagged. Yet the plastron is small, cross-shaped, and connected to the upper shell by narrow bridges.

I have known and studied the common snapping turtle for

many years. As a young boy, I had opportunity to familiarize myself with some of its behavior and breeding habits. More recently I have made observations on some of the feeding habits and other interesting activities of this species in its natural habitat.

# SNAPPING TURTLE
*(Chelydra serpentina serpentina)*

This large, ugly turtle is easily recognized by its quick temper and its willingness to defend itself with sharp, scissorlike jaws.

### Size and Body Structure

Although the shell of this turtle measures only about one and one-quarter inches when it emerges from the egg, snappers attain quite a larger size as adults. The average shell length of an adult is ten to fifteen inches, but they have been known to grow considerably larger.

Photo by the author

*plastron of the snapping ...le is somewhat cross-shaped ... is considerably reduced in ...parison to most other turtles.*

Mathewson (1955) reported a thirty-five pound snapping turtle from Staten Island, New York. Kauffeld (1949) reported another

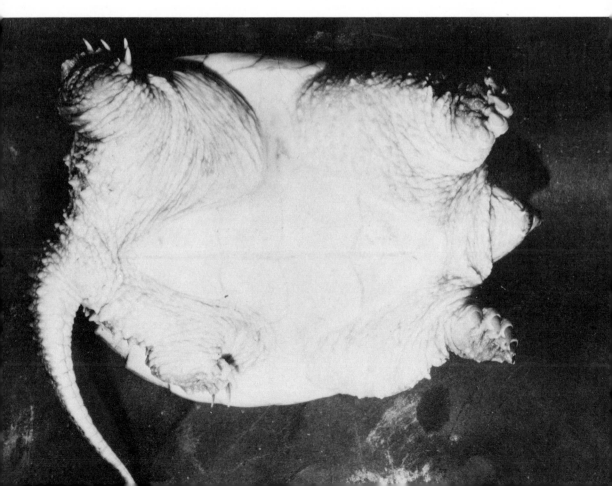

Staten Island specimen that weighed thirty-five pounds. In 1967 I collected a thirty-seven-pound individual at High Rock Park Conservation Center, which is in the "Green belt" area of Staten Island. The carapace length of this snapper was sixteen and one-quarter inches. Not only can we Staten Islanders boast of having the largest bridge in the United States, we can also boast of "giant" snapping turtles as well. Conant (1975) gives a record size of eighteen and one-half inches and a weight of thirty-five pounds. Also, Ernst and Barbour (1972) relate this information: "Adults may weigh more than seventy-five pounds. Males are known to grow much larger than females."

The carapace is large, well formed, and heavily serrated along the six posterior marginals. The upper shell of young individuals is extremely rough, with three low keels extending along the back in the form of knobby protrusions in the center of each scute. With age these "knobs" disappear, and old individuals have a smooth carapace. The plastron is somewhat cross-shaped and is considerably reduced in comparison to most other turtles. The fleshy underparts and limbs are largely exposed. The tail is very long, with a conspicuous "saw-toothed" dorsal crest, larger at the base and much smaller toward the tip. The head is also large, with the eyes located close to the snout; the eyes can be seen from

Photo by the au

*This photo clearly shows the* *spicuous paired fleshy barbel* *the chin of a snapping turtle.*

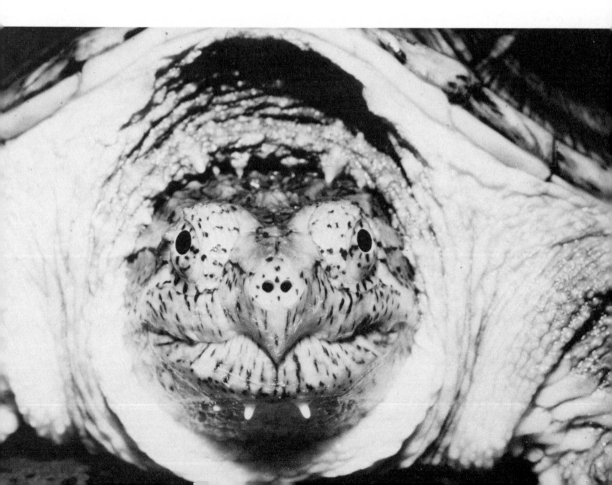

directly above the head. Scattered irregularly about the neck and underparts, there are many small blunt tubercles. The upper exposed surfaces of the limbs, especially the front ones, are protected by large, horny scales. Long toenails are typical of *Chelydra serpentina serpentina,* and are most pronounced on the males. Both the common snapping turtle and the Florida snapping turtle have conspicuous paired barbels on the chin.

### Coloration

The common snapping turtle is basically a rather drab, uncolorful turtle, but occasionally a brightly marked individual will turn up. I have seen a few specimens from Staten Island, New York, that had yellowish-gold lines radiating from the center of each scute, and light tan or orange on the face and lower neck. More typical snappers are usually some shade of dark gray, olive brown, or black. The plastron varies from a copperish-rust color to yellow, tan or almost white, with little or no pattern.

### Range

This prolific turtle enjoys a wide distribution over most of the United States east of the Rocky Mountains, from southern Canada to northern Florida and the Texas coast to Mexico. Introduced farther west, Degenhardt and Christiansen (1974) report *Chelydra serpentina serpentina* from New Mexico, at altitudes of 6700 feet. However, most other specimens taken during their study came from much lower altitude. Stebbins (1966) reports this species above 5000 feet in Colorado. This is a turtle that can thrive in almost any kind of aquatic habitat niche, getting along in a small shallow pond as well as a large, deep lake. This is by far the most common turtle on Staten Island, New York.

In Florida, there is a subspecies of *Chelydra,* called the Florida snapping turtle, *Chelydra serpentina osceoloa.* Although it looks quite similar to *Chelydra serpentina serpentina,* it has some distinct differences which have caused herpetologists to consider it a separate subspecies. These differences include elongated tubercles on the neck and three rows of saw-toothed scales on the tail, rather than one row as in the common snapper.

### Breeding Habits

Snappers spend the winter hibernating under the mud and don't emerge until springtime temperatures remain above 60° F. They have a long mating season that begins about mid-April and extends well into November. This of course varies with geographic location. A single male may mate more than once during the season, depending on the number of encounters he may have with mature, responsive females. I have seen snappers mate in the field as well as in captivity and have come to the conclusion that this species has no set pattern in its courtship behavior. On at least three occasions, I observed *Chelydra serpentina serpentina* mating in the wild. In all three cases the courtship behavior was slightly different.

In case number one, I saw a large snapping turtle swimming rather quickly along the bottom of a lake. It appeared to be chasing something, but I could not see what it was because of a thick clump of aquatic vegetation, since it was late in the summer (August 29, 1960). I did not think the turtle could be in the process of mating, but when I saw a smaller snapper swim out from beneath the matted vegetation with the larger one close behind, it was apparent that this was courtship behavior. The larger male caught up to the smaller female, and quickly made several savage bites at her head, neck and front limbs. Simultaneously he clamped down on the edges of her carapace with all four of his feet by hooking his claws under the marginals into the fleshy parts of her underside. He than began making a series of jerking movements with his tail, while he continued to bite at her head. This went on for a few minutes until the female made a violent attempt to swim upward towards the surface of the water. She succeeded in breaking the surface and quickly filled her lungs with air. The male took advantage of that moment and did the same. With her lungs filled, the female seemed to have more fight, and tried to retaliate by biting the male's head and front feet. With renewed enthusiasm, the male continued his aggressive action and soon had his tail under hers. They were joined for about ten minutes after which they swam their separate ways.

With observation number two, the precoital behavior was quite different. This took place in early spring (May 10, 1965). I was walking along the edge of a pond when I noticed two turtles moving along the bottom rather quickly. These proved to be a pair of snapping turtles in the process of courtship. Again the male was larger than the female. He was biting at the head and neck of the female, who offered little resistance. The male mounted the female, but she quickly started swimming and broke away. He swam after her and bit her on the neck, grasping a fold of loose skin and maintaining a hold on it. She again showed no resistance. This time the male was able to wrap his tail around hers, the mating lasting for about fifteen or twenty minutes.

Illustration by Florence W. Gibson

*ring the winter snapping
les dig down into the mud well
ow the frost line and lay
mant in hibernation. In some
es they use the runways of
skrats, or even burrow under-
th a muskrat's lodge. On
y occasions during the spring
l summer I used to capture
pping turtles by walking
ng muskrat runways and
ing under the banks with a
k. In order to find out if
ppers used the runways as a
ernaculum I checked this site
ing mid-winter and much to
surprise found five snappers
arious sizes hibernating in
skrat runways.*

The third observation was made in a very large lake on Staten Island, New York, on June 5, 1968. I was on a raft in search of painted turtles, *Chrysemys picta picta,* using a long-handled scoop net to capture them as they came to the surface for air. The depth of the water was about two and one-half feet, and the water was rather clear, permitting good visibility. I saw a couple of snapping turtles on the bottom of the pond, facing each other with the hind portions of their bodies elevated. Their front portions and necks touched the mud, with the heads fully extended and facing one another about two inches apart. Simultaneously, the two made sudden sideward sweeps of their heads in opposite directions, while moving slightly back and forth with their bodies. This was most puzzling to me for it was a behavior I had never seen before. At that moment I was not sure whether or not this was a combat dance of two male snappers or just some sort of unknown precoital behavior. It proved to be the latter. This head and neck movement lasted about five minutes; then the male advanced forward, spun around, and assumed the usual mating position. They were joined only about five minutes. I have seen similar matings in captivity, at the Staten Island Zoo.

During the spring, the zoo's American alligators were moved outdoors into their summer pool, leaving the indoor pool empty for other uses. It was used to exhibit several kinds of local turtles along with a few southern and exotic forms. Because the snapping turtle is so common on Staten Island, it is a species that is often brought to the zoo. Snappers are collected by young boys, or motorists pick them up as they cross roads. During a summer, we often receive as many as fifteen or twenty snappers of both sexes and various sizes, with a good portion of these being mature adults. These all have been placed together in the indoor turtle pool, along with other species of turtles, and released back into the wild again as soon as possible.

Over the years I have seen several snapping turtle matings take place, and for the most part, there was little variation in the courtship behavior, with only one exception. The following observation was made in late June, 1972. At that time we had only one large male (about twenty-five pounds) in the pool, along with an immature individual whose sex was undetermined. A man came to the reptile wing carrying a large cardboard box with a good-sized snapper in it. He said he found it crossing a road in a wooded section of Staten Island and was afraid it would be hit by a passing car, so he brought it to the zoo. This specimen proved to be an eighteen-pound female, but was without eggs. It was possible, however, that she had already laid them prior to her capture. At any rate, the female was introduced into the pool with the other turtles.

Typical of the way most turtles will react when first placed in a new enclosure, this female began to swim frantically about the pool. As she swam past the male, he seemed immediately to recognize her as a member of his own species, and of the opposite sex. This recognition was probably achieved by olfactory cues or by sight or by a combination of both. The female was picked up by the base of the tail and lowered into the pool; such handling will cause snappers to exude a strong musk from a gland located in the cloaca. The male quickly swam past the female, made a complete turn and stopped right in front of her. The female tried to slow down when she saw the male in front of her, but could not stop in time and collided with him. At that, the male began to snap at her face and front limbs. Suddenly she lowered the front portion of her body, raising her back legs and tail at the same time. Her head was fully extended, touching the floor of the pool, facing directly towards the male about one and one-half inches away. The male assumed the same position, with his snout facing the female's. He then began to make sideward sweeps with his head. The female started moving her head sideways, but in the opposite direction. They would stop for a moment or two, then continue for about eight to ten seconds more. This behavior lasted about three minutes, until the male swam over the female's back, grabbing her marginals with all four feet, and attempted to curl his tail under hers. Eventually, mating was achieved and lasting about ten minutes. These events were similar to observations I made in the field.

Upon searching the literature I've learned that other herpetologists have seen similar behavior with snapping turtles. J. M. Legler (1955) wrote a paper entitled: "Observations on the sexual behavior of turtles." Almost all the other matings I saw in the zoo's turtle pool, (and there were at least six), consisted of the typical aggressive behavior of the males. They chased after the females, as described before, biting at them and finally mounting them and copulation took place.

The gestation period varies from two to six weeks before egglaying occurs. It is interesting to note that it's possible for a female to lay more than one clutch of eggs, from the same mating, in a single season. Furthermore, the sperm may be stored in the genital tract of the female for the next couple of years, and continue to fertilize eggs in subsequent layings. However, the percentage of fertile eggs progressively decreases after the first

season. According to Smith (1956) "sperm may remain viable in
the female for several years."

### Egg-laying

Because *Chelydra serpentina serpentina* has such a long mating
season, egg-laying may occur anytime from late May through
mid-September. But the peak of the nesting season is around the
month of June; this was true at least on Staten Island, New York.
When a gravid female is about ready to lay her eggs, she crawls
out of the water onto the shore, and seeks a suitable nesting site.

Photo by the a

*Once a suitable site is select
the female snapper she beg
scrape out the nest chamber
alternate movements of her
feet.*

It is evident that this species shows no preference for the type of substrate in which the eggs are laid. I've found nests in sandy soil, rich top soil, rotting vegetation, and beneath sphagnum moss as well. These nests were dug at varing distances from the water's edge, and just why a female selects the particular spot she does is poorly understood by herpetologists. However, the character of the soil, as to moisture content and drainage, etc., may have something to do with the selection of the nesting site. Ernst and Barbour (1972) report the use of muskrat lodges as occasional nesting sites for snapping turtles. The closest I found snapper eggs to water was three feet, the farthest was several hundred feet in dry sandy soil.

Once a suitable site is selected by the female snapper she begins to scrape out the nest with alternate movements of the hind feet. Her long toenails play an important part in the scraping and digging of the nest, in hard or packed soil. The nest is usually flask-shaped, measuring from four to eight inches deep, depending on the size of the turtle. On top the opening is rather narrow, but slowly widens on an angle to a large nest chamber below. When the female is satisfied with the size and depth of the hole, egg-laying begins. The eggs are laid quickly at intervals of every half-minute to one minute apart. The lips of the vent are stretched considerably as the soft round egg is forced out. In some cases she then cups one of her back feet, catches and guides the egg to the floor of the chamber and this action reduces the impact as the egg hits the bottom. Each subsequent egg is guided into place by alternate motions of the hind feet. A clutch of eggs may contain anywhere from twelve to seventy-five eggs, although the average size clutch is about twenty to thirty. I once found a D.O.R. (dead on the road) female snapper that had fifty-three eggs inside of her.

The eggs are pinkish-white in color, and spherical in shape. These become tough and leathery an hour or so after laying. Snapping turtle eggs always reminded me of slightly smaller editions of ping-pong balls.

A large percentage of nests are destroyed by predators each year, but snappers survive because they lay so many eggs in comparison to some of the other smaller species. (The stinkpot, *sternotherus odoratus,* lays an average of two to five eggs; the bog turtle, *Clemmys muhlenbergi,* lays an average of only three eggs.) Many eggs on the bottom of the nesting chamber, are overlooked by predators and/or if a nest should go unmolested, the percentage of hatchings from that nest is high. This compensates for the nests that are destroyed by predators or the loss of hatches due to poor environmental conditions.

Snapping turtle eggs are eaten by a host of predators which includes mammals, birds, and other reptiles. Among the mammals the worst offenders are raccoons, skunks, foxes, and occasionally a mink or weasel. The worst of the bird predators are the crows, but grackles and starlings etc., will also take advantage of an open nest that has been disturbed by other predators. The eastern king snake, *Lampropeltis getulus getulus,* is one reptile predator that seems to show a definite preference for turtle eggs, in general, and if a king snake came across a female snapper in the process of laying eggs, it would probably have a field day eating them. Another snake known to feed on the eggs of the turtles, is the scarlet snake, *Cemophora coccinea.* This small snake punctures the eggshell with its pointed snout and laps up the egg. (Kaufield 1969)

After they are laid, the eggs hatch anywhere from 50 to 125 days later, depending on temperature, humidity and other environmental factors. Hatchling snappers, emerge from the eggs from mid-August to early October, however, if the cold weather arrives early, late egg clutches may not hatch until the following spring. In some cases, but not all, the eggs and/or the hatchlings

*The average size clutch is a 20 to 30 eggs. The author plac clutch of snapping turtle eggs glass fronted chamber in o to see how the hatchlings emer from the nest.*

may be killed by frost during the cold winter months if the eggs are above the frost line. If they are below the frost line, they will survive the winter, and emerge with the arrival of the warmer weather.

Hatchling *Chelydra serpentina serpentina* are small, about one inch or so, the carapace is nearly round in shape having three distinct keels. The tail is very long and tapers to a fine point. In fact, the tail is so long that it's longer than the turtle itself. This elongated tail is probably somewhat prehensile. Brode (1958) suggested that snappers may maintain their position in swift flowing streams by hooking their tails around fixed objects on the bottom. The upper shell is dark gray, rusty-brown or almost black with distinct light spots on the edge of each marginal. Newly-hatched individuals have a distinct buttonlike yolk sac in the center of the plastron and a light colored egg-tooth on the snout, but these disappear in one to three weeks.

Photo by the author

*ping turtle eggs hatch any-
e from 50 to 125 days after
g, depending on tempera-
humidity and other factors.
red here are a couple of
pers emerging from the
ical eggs.*

### Adult Behavior

Once the young snappers reach the safety of the water, they quickly burrow into the soft muck on the bottom of the stream,

pond or swamp, or seek shelter in some aquatic vegetation, or some other litter. Although they have rather good protective coloration it's important for them to remain inconspicuous because they now are exposed to several new predators which haven't bothered them while in the nest. They are now preyed upon by herons, bitterns and hawks, as well as bullfrogs and large fish.

### Diet

Young snapping turtles have a tremendous appetite, just as all small turtles have, and actively hunt for food which consists of both terrestrial and aquatic invertebrates, fish and fish eggs, frogs, toads and salamanders (including their eggs, larvae and tadpoles) as well as many kinds of crustaceans, (crayfish, fiddler crabs, shrimp, etc.). Carrion is also eaten. Although many people aren't aware of it, snapping turtles are actually omnivorous, and also feed on various algae, and many kinds of aquatic plants. Full-grown adult snappers can capture and overpower larger prey by dragging them beneath the water and holding on until they drown. This would include such animals such as muskrats, rice rats and other rodents, ducks (both adults and ducklings) and other birds, large fish, large bull frogs, water snakes, and other turtles.

They occasionally become cannibalistic. I have witnessed cannibalism among snapping turtles on at least two separate occasions. The first observation was made under captive conditions. In this case a large twelve-inch snapper ate a smaller four-inch cage companion, leaving only the head, part of the neck and the entire carapace. The rest of its carcass was not to be found in the tank because there was a tight fitting top on the tank, hence the only conclusion I could reach was that one turtle had eaten the other. At the time of this incident I shrugged it off as merely a quirk, some abnormal behavior that may have started with a fight over food. They had plenty of food to eat, however, so I really couldn't account for why it happened, refusing to believe that it was actually cannibalistic behavior. I also took into consideration the fact that an animal in captivity doesn't necessarily behave or react the same way as one in the wild. Nevertheless, I didn't give it much thought until some years later, when I made a similar observation in the field. It took place on July 5th in the summer of 1958, while walking alongside a shallow, slow-moving stream near my home in Charleston, Staten Island.

It was a warm sunny day, with a temperature of about 78°

Fahrenheit and many green frogs, *Rana clamitans melanota,* were sitting along the bank of the stream, jumping into the water as I approached. An occasional pickerel frog, *Rana palustris,* would also leap frantically through the tall foxtail grass, disappearing out of sight. A plump water snake, *Natrix sipedon sipedon,* slithered silently from an overhanging branch into the trickling water. Suddenly, something caught my eye just ahead of me in the stream. It was a good-sized snapper (about eight inches) in the process of eating something. Much to my surprise, it was feeding on a smaller snapping turtle (about three inches). The large snapper had the smaller turtle flipped over on its carapace, and was tearing off a piece of its front leg and plastron with its sharp scissor-like jaws. The head, neck, right front leg and part of the plastron had already been eaten. I quietly watched as the snapper devoured one of its own kind; it left only the empty carapace. Once it saw me standing there, it quickly made an effort to escape, but I picked it up to examine it. This was a healthy individual that reacted in true snapper fashion, emitting a strong musk and snapping violently at me.

As I looked at the turtle, I tried to theorize why it attacked the other snapper. Was this turtle just an "oddball," or was it behaving like the average snapper would? I probably would have thought this was exceptional rather than normal behavior if it weren't for the fact that this was the second time I witnessed cannibalistic behavior with *Chelydra serpentina serpentina.* This particular turtle fed on whatever food was available in the stream environment it was living in. In this case it happened to be a smaller member of its own race. The next meal the turtle might find would probably be a frog or large earthworm. To the turtle it's all the same; it has to eat to survive, and it will eat a small, immature snapping turtle, as well as any of the other animals it preys upon.

Once a snapper reaches twelve inches or more, there are very few animals that will prey upon them. In the southeastern part of the United States however, even full-grown adults aren't safe from the American alligator, *Alligator mississippiensis,* for they are notorious turtle eaters. A large gator will easily kill and eat a full-grown snapping turtle that weighs twenty pounds or more. I once experimented at the Staten Island Zoo to find out if alligators will attack and eat large snappers in captivity.

We had two snappers that were injured by automobiles on a roadway. Their weight was twenty pounds and twenty-four pounds, respectively. Before placing the turtles in the pool, I wanted to be sure the alligators had full stomachs. They are always fed on Sunday afternoon, so I waited until Monday morning. As the turtles swam around they quickly attracted the attention of some of the alligators and both were captured with a sudden side sweep of a gator's broad powerful jaws. It wasn't long before they were both dead, their shells riddled with punctures and cracks from gator teeth. As the afternoon approached no trace of either turtle was to be found.

Although alligators may occasionally eat snapping turtles, man is by far their worst predator. They are hunted and killed for meat throughout their entire range for a tasty soup can be made from the flesh, and their fresh eggs are edible if fried.

Snappers are probably one of the most versatile of all the turtles, being able to survive in any kind of aquatic environment from an old well or small pond to a large lake or river. As long as there is an adequate food supply available to them, they will remain at that pond or lake. However, if the food supply becomes too low, they migrate to another suitable habitat and sometimes over long distances. I once found an eight-inch snapping turtle walking along a sand road in the Pine Barrens of southern New Jersey. The nearest source of water that I knew of was a stream about one mile away, but the turtle was walking *away* from it. There was a large lake, about one and one-half miles further down the road in the direction the turtle was walking, but I didn't think it would have made it because of the high temperature—about 85° Fahrenheit that day. So I picked the turtle up, and dropped it off at the lake where it seemed very happy to be put in the water. When a snapping turtle finds a stream or pond with a suitable food supply, it probably remains there for an indefinite period. They usually become somewhat territorial, having their same daily feeding grounds, and favorite basking spots. Some snappers lie under a muddy bank or log to ambush their prey, others go out and hunt actively.

In most cases, but not all, snapping turtles are bottom-baskers, but they occasionally climb out of the water to bask when infested with blood-sucking leeches. The only way they can rid themselves of these parasites is by completely drying out in the warm sun until the leeches drop off.

Snapping turtles seem to show a preference for ponds with muddy bottoms or streams with overhanging banks. I've often found them in muskrat runways, or tunnels under the muskrat lodge. I once recaptured the same individual several times, in the same muskrat runway during the course of the summer of 1962. From time to time, other specimens were found with this marked individual, but for the most part they never returned again. In early spring the following year, the same snapper was found in its regular spot, under the runway, which made it seem probable that the turtle hibernated there.

### General Discussion

Most snapping turtles can bite savagely and will do so with little provocation. When first captured they emit a potent musk, equal to if not worse than the stinkpot *Sternotherus odoratus,* and snap at anything that comes near them. They should be treated with respect and handled with care because they can inflict a serious wound. Never try to pick up a snapper by the sides of the shell as you would with most other turtles, because they can reach around with their long necks and bite.

The proper way to handle an adult snapper is to pick it up by the back limbs, with the plastron facing towards you, but well

Photo by Zigmund Leszczynski

*The author demonstrates how to carry an adult snapping turtle: pick it up by the back limbs, with the plastron facing towards you, but well away from the body. Carrying one by the tail may severely injure the turtle.*

away from the body. Never carry large snapping turtles by the tail for any prolonged period; this can severely injure them by separating the caudal vertebrae; the weight of the body will also effect the sacral region by stretching it. They can be picked up by the tail, when pulling them out of the water in capturing them, until a better grip on the legs can be accomplished, or in the case of an emergency for quick handling.

The snapping turtle is a useful and interesting reptile and plays an important part in the ecology of the pond, lake or stream environment it lives in, although they may occasionally take a game fish or waterbird. Under natural conditions, the snapper occupies its niche in the balance of nature, probably doing more good than harm by acting as bottom-prowling carrion eaters.

# ALLIGATOR SNAPPING TURTLE
### (Macroclemys temmincki)

The alligator snapping turtle is the only living member of the genus. They are the largest freshwater turtles in the United States, and among one of the largest turtles of the freshwater species in the world. Even though they are known to attain such a large size, little is really known about their everyday behavior and movements in the natural habitat. The reasons for this lack of knowledge are two-fold; first, nowhere in its range is the alligator snapping turtle considered to be a common species. Secondly, due to their secretive, deep-water, bottom-prowling habits and the fact that they seldom, if ever, bask, they are a most difficult turtle to study in the wild.

Because of their basic similarity in physical appearance and body structure, most amateurs often confuse the common snapping turtle with the alligator snapping turtle. Although the two species may look alike at first glance, closer examination reveals distinct differences. These distinguishing characteristics are easily noticeable once they are pointed out (see photo).

### Size and Body Structure

The average adult size of this species ranges from about fifteen to twenty-five inches at weights of thirty to fifty pounds. The largest individual on record is one that was exhibited in Chicago's Brookfield Zoo. It tipped the scale at 236 pounds (Minton and Minton

Photo by Jack Muntzner

e alligator snapping turtle the
rgest freshwater turtle known
occur in the United States, is
own here side by side with a
mmon snapping turtle. Notice
e difference in the structure of
e shell; the alligator snapper
s three prominent dorsal keels
tending along the entire upper
ell, whereas the common
apper has a smooth carapace
an adult.

1973). Another giant alligator snapper was reported by Conant
(1958); this specimen weighed 219 pounds. Such large alligator
snapping turtles aren't at all common in zoos. Although there
still may be some of these giants left in the Mississippi River,
finding and capturing such monsters is not very likely.

The major identifying characteristics of the alligator snapping
turtle follow. When viewing *Macroclemys temminckii* from directly above the head, the eyes cannot be seen, whereas with
*Chelydra serpentina serpentina* and *Chelydra serpentina osceola*,
they can be seen from that position. Adult *Macroclemys temminckii* as well as the young have a huge, pointed head, a strongly
hooked jaw, and three prominent dorsal keels extending along
the full length of the upper shell. Both other species of snapping
turtles have a smooth carapace as adults. The most outstanding
characteristic which *Macroclemys temmincki* has is the extra
row of scutes called supramarginals located on both sides of
carapace between the first three pleural scutes and the marginals. They usually number from three to eight; these are entirely

lacking with the common and Florida snapping turtles. Most other body and shell characteristics are similar to the two snappers of the genus *Chelydra*.

### Coloration

The carapace is a rusty, dark brown, mahogany or dark gray with no markings. Its colors match that of the muddy river bottom.

Photo by Jack Munt

*Very little is known about courtship, mating and nestin this secretive giant. They sta the water most of the time seldom bask, except in shal water. As a result, the carap is usually covered with a th growth of algae, thus winn them the name "moss-backs".*

### Breeding Habits

Very little is known about the courtship, mating and nesting of this species. The only information available, was some observations made by Allen and Neill (1950) on some captive pairs under semi-natural conditions. To my knowledge most of their breeding habits are quite similar to that of *Chelydra serpentina serpentina*. one major difference, however, is that female alligator snappers only come out of water to deposit eggs, and are otherwise almost never away from it. The males presumably never venture out on land; this factor was true of the individuals we had over the years at the Staten Island Zoo.

### Range

The alligator snapper is chiefly a river or deep-water turtle occurring in the Mississippi Valley river system from Illinois, Iowa and Kansas southward to the Gulf states and it also ranges on the coastal plain from southeastern Georgia and northern Florida west to eastern Texas.

Photo by Zigmund Leszczynski

*author showing the safest hod of handling an adult alli- or snapping turtle.*

### Adult Behavior

It is probable, that this secretive turtle ventures into shallow water in order to bask, but never in water so shallow that the carapace would be above the water surface. This type of basking would account for the thick growths of algae on their upper shell. Many Southerners often refer to them as "moss-backs" because of

the heavy deposits of green algae that often covers their carapace
and the upper surfaces of their head and tail. Some superstitious
and misinformed river people believe that the alligator snapping
turtle originated from a freak of nature when an American alligator and a common snapping turtle mated, thus producing the
alligator snapper. This, of course, is not so.

The alligator snapping turtle has basically the same feeding
habits as the snappers of the genus *Chelydra,* but with one important difference. That lies in the way in which they capture some of
their prey during the daylight hours. They are remarkably equipped with a special lure to entrap unwary fish and small turtles.

Photo by Jack Muntzi

*Notice the worm-like lure on*
*tongue that is used to attract fi*
*and small turtles. When some u*
*expecting fish swims into the tr*
*their powerful jaws snap shut.*

This wormlike lure, located on the tongue in the floor of the mouth, is used to attract the attention of their prey. *Macroclemys* sits motionless with mouth gaped wide open under the concealment of an overhanging bank or tree stump. It then sets into motion the curious, worm-shaped process. Eventually some unsuspecting turtle or fish, will notice the lure and swim into the mouth, only to have the turtle's powerful jaws snap shut. Smaller prey is swallowed whole, whereas larger victims are crushed by the strong, sharp jaws. The alligator snapping turtle is the only turtle known to have this kind of amazing feeding adaptation.

# Chapter 5

# MUSK AND MUD TURTLES

Turtles belonging to this family (family Kinosternidae) are small to medium in size, with pointed snouts and very small tails. Most have a smooth, egg-shaped carapace and a single or double-hinged plastron.

This New World family has representatives occurring from southern Canada, southward through most of the United States, Mexico, Central America and South America. There are 23 species within this family, consisting of four genera—most of these are Central and South American. Of the four genera known to science, two of these occur in the United States: *Kinosternon,* the mud turtles, and *Sternotherus,* the musk turtles.

The genus *Kinosternon* contains 16 species of which five are found in this country, and have been fairly well studied, whereas most of the Central and South American species have been subject to very little research and their habits and life histories are almost completely unknown.

Closely related to the mud turtles, is the genus *Sternotherus* which is represented in this country by three species. Two of the three species are restricted to the United States, however, the Stinkpot, *Sternotherus odoratus,* which is the most widespread and common of all the musk turtles, is also found in southern

Canada and northern Mexico. This genus received its common name from the odor produced from musk glands on each side of the body, near the bridge.

## MUSK TURTLES (Genus *Sternotherus*)

Because of their ability to exude a strong, unpleasant smelling secretion from their musk glands when captured or disturbed, the musk turtles have earned such inelegant names as "stinkpots" or "stinking jims." The musk glands are located at the edge of the shell, where the skin meets the carapace, by either side of the bridge.

Most amateurs often confuse musk turtles, *Sternotherus,* with

Photo by the author

*...usk turtles,* Sternotherus *...eratus, have a single frontal ...ge and pectoral shields that ...e somewhat squarish in shape.*

mud turtles, *Kinosternon,* mistaking one for the other. The best way to distinguish the two is by checking for the following characteristics. Must turtles have:

(1) A relatively small, fleshy plastron, that gives little protection to the limbs.
(2) Only one frontal hinge on the plastron.
(3) Their pectoral scutes, near the hinge on the plastron, are somewhat squarish in shape.

An account of the musk turtles in the United States, including their subspecies follows:

(1) Stinkpot, *Sternotherus odoratus*
(2) Razorbacked Musk Turtle, *Sternotherus carinatus*
(3) The Loggerhead Musk Turtles. Three subspecies have been described:
  (A) Loggerhead Musk Turtle, *Sternotherus minor minor*
  (B) Striped-necked Musk Turtle, *Sternotherus minor peltifer*
  (C) Flattened Musk Turtle, *Sternotherus minor depressus*

Of the species listed above, the one I'm most familiar with is the stinkpot or common musk turtle, having observed it in the field and kept them successfully in captivity.

# THE STINKPOT
### (Sternotherus odoratus)

### Size and Body Structure

These are usually dull, moss-covered three-and-a-half to four-and-a-half inch turtles. The record size reached by this species is five and three-eights inches (Conant 1975).

Stinkpots are easily recognized by two prominent yellowish-white stripes on the sides of the head. These usually start at the pointed snout and pass above and below the eyes. The lower stripe then slopes slightly downward with the angle of the jaw. Both extend onto the neck; these may or may not be broken and discontinuous. Look also for the presence of paired barbels on the chin and throat (small, fleshy downward projections). The smooth carapace is highly arched, somewhat elongated and rather narrow. Young individuals have a rough carapace with a prominent mid-dorsal keel, but this is gradually lost with age. The scutes of the carapace usually don't overlap one another except with very young individuals.

Photo by the author

*kpots, Sternotherus oderatus, uent an assortment of habitats h as slow-moving streams, ds, lakes, canals and swamps. stinkpot is a highly aquatic ies spending most of its time ching the bottom of the pond tream for carrion. They often l bait from the hooks of erman.*

### *Coloration*

In general, the carapace varies from light to dark brown, gray or black, but the color is sometimes obscured by deposits of thick green algae on the upper parts of the shell. The plastron ranges from tan, yellow, orange or brown with broad areas of skin showing between the scutes. These skin patches are most pronounced on the males. Males also have longer, thicker tails that end with a blunt terminal nail. Females have much shorter tails. The head, neck, limbs and fleshy underparts are black to light gray in color.

### *Range*

*Sternotherus odoratus* has a wide range from southern Canada (Ontario) and New England southward to Florida, west to Wisconsin and central Texas. More recently, there have been scattered records of stinkpots occurring in south-central Kansas, and

Chihuahua, Mexico. Similar to the snapping turtles of the genus *Chelydra,* stinkpots frequent an assortment of habitats such as slow-moving streams, ponds, lakes, canals and swamps. They seem to show a preference for the more shallow waters of their respective environments, basking and feeding in these places for hours at a time. However, there is a report of a specimen taken in water thirty feet deep (Carr 1940, 1952).

### Breeding Habits

Stinkpots mate throughout the year, whenever mature adults encounter one another. However, the peak of the mating season usually occurs in the spring, around April or May. Males tend to be far more active in their endeavor to seek females at this time, crawling about the bottom of the lake or stream with necks and head fully extended in search of a female.

Most of my observations on the behavior and breeding habits of *Sternotherus odoratus* were made in the Pine Barrens of southern New Jersey, over a period of several years.

In May of 1968, I found a pair of stinkpots mating on the bottom of a stream, at a depth of three feet. They were well into the second part of the courtship behavior. Most turtles have at least three phases to their courtship pattern; recognition and precoital behavior is the first phase. This usually consists of the male prowling about the bottom in search of a mate. When another stinkpot is encountered, the male smells it along the side and about the tail to determine its sex. If it's a female, courtship continues; if it's another male, the two go off on their separate ways. The second part of the courtship is mounting and copulation. When mounting a receptive female, the male approaches her from behind and quickly climbs onto her carapace and positions himself with his plastron more or less on the center of her shell, then hooks the edge of her marginals with all four feet. At the same time, he works his thick, blunt tail beneath hers, and bites at her head and front limbs. Once the proper angle is achieved, mating takes place. The third phase of the courtship consists of nudging, rubbing and sometimes biting. The pair of musk turtles I observed were joined for about ten minutes. For the most part, the female was passive throughout. Male stinkpots have two small patches of rough, scaly skin on the inner surfaces of each hind leg. These scaly patches aren't present on females, so some herpetologists believe they play a part in aiding the males to maintain a grip on the tail of the female while mating.

### Egg-laying

The egg-laying season varies with geographic location, but usually occurs around the end of May and throughout the month of June in the Pine Barrens. Most of the nests I've found were along high, sandy stream banks. Predators had dug up many of the nests and eaten the eggs. In most cases raccoon tracks and droppings were present around the destroyed nests, but the tracks of skunks and crows were also there occasionally. On one occasion I found a destroyed nest in a rotten pine log by the edge of a lake. There were many broken eggshells, numbering at least sixteen, so this was probably a nesting site where several females had deposited their eggs. The average-size clutch of a female stinkpot is about four eggs, but larger specimens may lay as many as eight. Younger females only lay one or two fertile eggs. The average size of the eggs is just about one inch in length, but many are somewhat smaller. The incubation period is about 60 days, depending on environmental factors. Hatchings emerge from the nest around the beginning of September and are an inch or so in length. At this time the color of the carapace is black and of rough texture, with a prominent mid-dorsal keel. Most have a light spot on each marginal, and the face and head stripes are distinct.

### Adult Behavior

Stinkpots are highly aquatic in habits, spending most of their time parading about the bottom of the pond or stream in search of food, or sometimes resting on aquatic plants with the top of the carapace exposed to the sun. However, most bask in shallow water within an inch or so of the surface. They are also known to climb out onto the banks of the stream, or on a stump or fallen tree to bask occasionally. Conant (1975) remarked on the tendency for *Sternotherus odoratus* to climb as high as six feet above the surface of the water. I too have observed this; on many occasions, I've seen them dropping off the blueberry bushes and cedar trees that grow so close to the edge of the streams throughout the Pine Barrens. Incidentally, I was once hit on the shoulder by a stinkpot, when it dropped off a cedar tree as I passed beneath it.

Musk turtles are omnivorous in their feeding habits, young individuals usually feed on all sorts of aquatic insects along with earthworms, snails and algae. Adults feed on carrion, crayfish, crabs, snails, clams, leeches, insects, fish and their eggs, tadpoles, frogs, algae and other aquatic vegetation. It's interesting to note that stinkpots seem to show a tendency to congregate in large numbers. In one area that was only six-feet wide along a narrow stream, I once collected eight specimens. On another occasion, my colleague Jim Bockowski and I found a dozen stinkpots under a small bridge. These ranged in size from about two to five inches, with the largest individual being a male. We found them so numerous in one stream that we were catching two or three turtles with each scoop of the net. Between us, Jim holds the record, having once caught four juveniles in one scoop. This area always yielded musk turtles, but I have never seen them as plentiful as they were on that occasion. Most fishermen are familiar with this turtle because they often are caught while trying to steal bait from their hooks.

## MUD TURTLES (Genus *Kinosternon*)

Mud turtles can quickly be distinguished from musk turtles by the following characteristics—mud turtles have:

1. A large plastron in comparision to a musk turtle, which offers almost complete protection to the head and limbs when they are withdrawn into the shell.
2. Two readily noticeable transverse hinges on the plastron.
3. Their pectoral scutes, near the front hinge on the plastron, are somewhat triangular in shape.

An account of the mud turtles of the United States, including their subspecies:

1. The Eastern Mud Turtles, three subspecies are recognized:
    A. Eastern Mud Turtle, *Kinosternon suburbrum suburbrum*
    B. Mississippi Mud Turtle, *Kinosternon suburbrum hippocrepis*
    C. Florida Mud Turtle, *Kinosternon suburbrum steindachneri*
2. The Striped Mud Turtles; two subspecies have been described:
    A. Key Mud Turtle, *Kinosternon bauri bauri*
    B. Striped Mud Turtle, *Kinosternon baurii palmarum*
3. The Yellow Mud Turtles; three subspecies are recognized:
    A. Yellow Mud Turtle, *Kinosternon flavescens flavescens*
    B. Mexican Yellow Mud Turtle, *Kinosternon flavescens stejnegeri*
    C. Illinois Mud Turtle, *Kinosternon flavescens spooneri*
4. Sonora Mud Turtle, *Kinosternon sonoriense*

Photo by the author

*An adult female bog turtle,* Clemmys muhlenbergi, *parading about a sphagnum bog in search for food in the afternoon sun.*

Photo by the author

*The convex plastron of this adult female has a bold yellowish center figure.*

Photo by the author

*The deep orange head blotch of this New Jersey bog turtle is exceptionally large.*

Photo by Saul Friess
*The large, distinctive head-blotch is quite noticeable on this small bog turtle.*

Photo by the author
*A typical marshy habitat of* Clemmys muhlenbergi. *These kind of areas are destroyed and filled-in for roads, housing projects or farm land—all too often without proper wildlife studies beforehand.*

Photo by Zigmund Leszczynski
*After recording all pertinent data, the author is preparing to release a pair of bog turtles back into the wild*

*This adult female eastern box turtle,* Terrapene c. carolina, *shows that red eyes are not restricted to males alone. I have found several red-eyed females on my collecting trips over the years.*

*Eastern box turtles exhibit a wide array of colors and patterns on both the carapce and the plastron as the picture clearly shows.*

*Hatchling eastern box turtles are shy and secretive, and are not often encounted in the field. They feed on a variety of small animals and invertebrates.*

*A Mississippi map turtle,* Grap-temys kohni, *basking on the bank of a river. These predominantly aquatic turtles will dive into the water with astonishing speed when alarmed.*

*An adult eastern painted turtle,* Chrysemys picta picta, *sunning itself on a rock. Males do not grow as large as females and have long front toenails which are used in courtship behavior.*

*This adult female eastern painted turtle displays her beautiful yellow head markings.*

5. Rough-footed Mud Turtles; two races are recognized:
   - A. Rough-footed Mud Turtle, *Kinosternon hirtipes hirtipes*
   - B. Big Bend Mud Turtle, *Kinosternon hirtipes murrayi*

Of the five species of *Kinosternon* listed above, the one I'm most familiar with is the eastern mud turtle, *Kinosternon subrubrum subrubrum*. It's a species I have collected as a youngster on Staten Island, New York, and one which I've collected throughout its range in the eastern United States.

Photo by the author

*mud turtle,* Kinosternon rubrum subrubrum, *has a ge plastron with two trans- e hinges and pectoral shields t are somewhat triangular in pe.*

# EASTERN MUD TURTLE
*(Kinosternon subrubrum subrubrum)*

### Size and Body Structure

These small trutles reach sexual maturity at about three or four inches, which is the average size of this species, but Conant (1958, 1975) gives a record size of four and seven-eighths inches. In April of 1973, I found an empty mud turtle shell in a swamp in southern South Carolina that also measured four and seven-eighths inches; this shell was turned over to the Museum of Natural History in New York.

Their carapace is smooth, low and unkeeled, with no distinctive pattern or markings. The head is well proportioned with a strongly hooked snout, a pair of barbels are present on the chin, with a second, but smaller pair on the neck. Their limbs are stout and muscular, with webbing on each foot. Females have short, stubby tails whereas males have much longer thicker tails that end with a terminal nail. Males also have two small patches of rough scales on the inner portion of each hind leg.

Photo by the

*The mud turtle is a shy and tive species, but after heavy they often parade about l for better feeding grounds.*

### Coloration

The carapace of a typical eastern mud turtle is usually some shade of brown, but I've seen them vary from dark yellow, orange, maroon and even black. The plastron is usually yellowish-brown, with some darker coloring between the scutes; their limbs, neck and fleshy underparts are brownish-gray. Most have yellowish markings on the sides of the head, that sometimes form lines which extend to the neck.

### Range

*Kinosternon subrubrum subrubrum* has a rather wide range in the eastern United States from southwestern Connecticut, Long Island and Staten Island, to the Gulf Coast of Florida; it also ranges into Kentucky, southern Indiana and Illinois. This is a wandering species that seems to show a preference for shallow water such as roadside ditches, marshes, small temporary ponds, wet meadows, and brackish tidal waters. They often wander across roads in early morning or late afternoon in search of food or better water.

### Breeding Habits

On Staten Island, New York, the breeding season usually begins around mid-April and extends through May and early June, but probably occurs in late spring and early summer throughout the rest of the range, depending on geographic location. On May 10, 1958, I found a pair of mud turtles joined in a small pond at a depth of one foot. The male was biting and nudging the female's head; she offered little or no resistance, however, once released, she quickly fled.

### Egg-laying

June is the egg-laying season for this species; this was at least true of the populations I studied on Staten Island, New York and in the Pine Barrens of southern New Jersey.

Some good friends of mine, Chris and Tony DeFranco, made some interesting observations on the egg-laying habits of *Kinosternon subrubrum subrubrum* in the Pine Barrens of southern New Jersey. In June, 1973, they made several trips to an area where turtles were known to nest, in order to observe their nesting behavior. They found one place of particular interest, a sand road cut along the edge of a large lake on one side and bordering a brackish, salt march on the other side. Many species of turtles use this road to deposit their eggs, because it's the highest ground for a mile or so in any direction.

During the course of a season, the following freshwater turtles were seen laying eggs along the shoulder of the road: eastern mud turtle, *Kinosternon subrubrum subrubrum;* spotted turtle, *Clemmys guttata;* eastern painted turtle, *Chrysemys picta picta;* red-bellied turtle, *Chrysemys rubriventris rubriventris;* and snapping turtle, *Chelydra serpentina serpentina.* They also found one box turtle, *Terrapene carolina carolina,* nest at the end of the road, close to the woods. From the salt marsh, the northern diamondback terrapin, *Malaclemys terrapin terrapin,* also came up the road to nest. Many predators were attracted to this site because of the large number of turtles that nested there. Raccoons and skunks were the worst offenders, but opossum, muskrat, crows, herons and king snakes were also seen.

Most of the mud turtles were seen nesting in the early morning, but on one occasion they found a female constructing a nest in late afternoon. In most cases, after a short search, the female began to dig the nest with her front feet. The sand was pushed out with alternate motions of the feet, until the turtle was almost completely out of sight. She then came out of the nest and backed in, tail first. Only the head of the turtle was visible at this time. Once the eggs were laid, the female crawled out of the nest and only partially covered the eggs, before returning to the water. Three of the nests they examined contained eggs—four in two of the nests, and five in the other. One nest found on the following day, had only two eggs in it. The small eggs are about one inch in size; they are pinkish-white with an extremely brittle shell. In late August and September, the hatchlings emerge after an incubation period of about 75 days.

### Adult Behavior

On Staten Island, I've found mud turtles in small ponds with muddy bottoms and lots of aquatic vegetation, or in muddy, overgrown streams. Occasionally I found juvenile specimens basking on boards, or at the water's edge. They seem to like soft bottoms or streams with overhanging banks which they hide under. I've collected mud turtles in New York, New Jersey, Maryland, North Carolina, South Carolina and Georgia, and noticed no difference in their behavior.

In South Carolina while hunting for snakes in "stump holes", it was a common occurrence to find mud turtles sitting in the openings of the stumps. I would also find them under logs, or just walking across the wet fields. Many of these fields are flooded during the winter and spring, and they begin to dry up around April. The mud turtles must estivate until heavy rains come, allowing them some activity again. In Maryland, I've found several mud turtles in brackish tidal streams. These were seen feeding on dead fish and snails. Similar to the musk turtles, mud turtles also steal bait from the hooks of fishermen.

# Chapter 6

# AQUATIC, SEMIAQUATIC AND BOX TURTLES

Family Emydidae has some of the most colorful and diverse kinds of turtles in the world. In fact, it's the largest family of living turtles known to science; containing twenty-five genera and more than eighty species with representatives on all major continents except Australia.

In the United States the family Emydidae has seven genera with about twenty-five species. Most members are medium to large in size with bright colors and patterns. All have a well developed carapace, bridge and plastron. A few genera have a movable hinge on the plastron that can be closed tightly for full protection of the head and limbs. The more highly aquatic forms have strongly webbed feet, whereas the semiaquatic species have feet that are only feebly webbed. The few terrestrial kinds entirely lack webbing between their toes.

Because this is such a large and diverse United States family it's difficult to summerize them in this chapter. Instead, there will be listed all the genera represented in the family, with a full account of the United States species together with the typical life histories and behavior of a few of the most oustanding turtles in this family.

The seven genera that occur in the United States are:

1. *Clemmys:* The Semiaquatic Pond, Bog and Wood Turtles

2. *Terrapene:* The Box Turtles
3. *Malaclemys:* The Salt-Marsh, Diamondback Terrapins
4. *Graptemys:* The Map Turtles
5. *Chrysemys:* The Painted Turtles and their relatives
6. *Deirochelys:* The Chicken Turtles
7. *Emydoidae:* The Blanding's Turtle

## SEMIAQUATIC POND TURTLES (Genus *Clemmys*)

The genus *Clemmys* is restricted to North America. It's a very old genus, as fossil records have shown, that first evolved sometime during the Paleocene epoch some 75 million years ago. Four species of *Clemmys* occur in the United States.

Three of these are found in the northeastern states, and one species is restricted to the Pacific Coast. The name semiaquatic truly fits the turtles belonging to this complex. They have long, muscular legs and most have poorly webbed feet which indicates they are somewhat terrestrial and not totally adapted to life in water. However, all are excellent swimmers, and are just as at home in the water as out of it.

### An Account of the Species

1. Spotted Turtle, *Clemmys guttata*
2. Bog Turtle, *Clemmys muhlenbergi*
3. Wood Turtle, *Clemmys insculpta*
4. The Western Pond Turtles; two subspecies are recognized:
   A. Northwestern Pond Turtle, *Clemmys marmorata marmorata*
   B. Southwestern Pond Turtle, *Clemmys marmorata pallida*

The life history and behavior of the Bog Turtle, *Clemmys muhlenbergi,* which appears under the next heading is given as an example of the *Clemmys* group. This turtle was chosen because very little was known about its basic biology. Since its discovery back in the late 18th century, most of the information concerning this species dealt with its distribution and range, and/or range extensions. Almost nothing has been printed on its behavior, and breeding habits in the natural habitat.

For many years the *Clemmys* complex has been one of my favorite groups of turtles; of these the bog turtle has always held for me a particular interest. In the spring of 1972 I began serious

research on this species in the hope of discovering the secrets that
have long surrounded this handsome little turtle. In 1973, 1974,
and 1975, my studies were supported in part, by the Research
Grants Allocation Committee of the National Audubon Society,
the Highlands Biological Station, in North Carolina (1975 only),
and the Staten Island Zoological Society.

### History and Nomenclature

The bog turtle has a long and interesting history that dates back
to the American Revolution. At that time a Hessian Regiment
was fighting with the colonists in Pennsylvania. Attached to the
regiment was a German physician and naturalist by the name of

Photo by the

*A female spotted turtle, Cle*
*guttata, basking on a log.*
*is a common species fou*
*marshy places throughou*
*eastern United States from*
*ern Maine to northern Flor*

Photo by the author

*s female bog turtle,* Clemmys *lenbergi, has just climbed a grassy tussock, which is red with a thick, green carpet phagnum moss, to bask in the ning sun.*

Johann David Schoepff who was serving as a surgeon. While Schoepff was in Philadelphia in 1778 he made the acquaintance of Heinreich Muhlenberg, a clergyman and botanist from Lancaster, Pennsylvania. Rev. Muhlenberg collected an assortment of turtles in the streams and bogs of Lancaster County, Pennsylvania, which he presented to Dr. Schoepff. From among these turtles Schoepff described a new and unknown species, giving its type location as Lancaster County, Pennsylvania. In 1801 he published this information in a paper called "Historia Testudinum"—this was printed in his native language, German. The turtle was named Muhlenberg's tortoise, *Testudo muhlenbergii,* in honor of its discoverer, Heinreich Muhlenberg.

In the years that followed, the turtle was discovered in other areas of southwestern Pennsylvania, and in the state of New Jersey as well. The Muhlenberg's tortoise was reclassified by another German naturalists, L. J. Fitzinger, in 1835. Fitzinger transferred it to the genus *Clemmys* where it still remains today. The following year, 1836, one of our pioneer herpetologists, Dr. John Edwards Holbrook, wrote a paper entitled "North American

Photo by Zigmund Leszczy

*The wood turtle,* Clemr
insculpta, *the largest membe*
*the* Clemmys complex, *o*
*reaches a shell length of se*
*inches. They range from N*
*Scotia to eastern Minnesota*
*southward to Virginia in the E*

Herpetology; a description of the reptiles inhabiting the United States." Included in Holbrook's paper was a description and line drawing of the bog turtle. Even then in 1836, the turtle was considered rare. Holbrook gives this information: "Its range is very limited; being only found in New Jersey and East Pennsylvania, and rare even in these districts." It wasn't discovered in any other states at the time of Holbrook's writing.

Eventually, a colony was discovered in the state of New York by a naturalist named J. W. Hill. In the early part of May, Hill collected a pair of bog turtles in the meadows of Clarkstown in Rockland County, New York, and gave them to James E. De Kay, a New York herpetologist. In 1842, De Kay wrote a paper entitled: "Zoology of New York, New York Fauna." The paper was written in three parts, with part three dealing with the reptiles and amphibia. This was the first publication reporting that bog turtles occurred in New York State.

De Kay gave a detailed description of the turtle and also provided an accurate line drawing. As time passed other localities in New York State also were discovered. On September 2, 1902, a bog turtle was found near Silver Lake, Staten Island, New York by Mr. A. B. Skinner, before the lake was turned into a reservoir. Mr. Skinner gave this specimen to William T. Davis, a famous entomologist and naturalist affiliated with the Staten Island Museum. This was a single adult female, the first reported from Staten Island, so there was some question as to whether or not this specimen was indigenous or one that was liberated. The question remained unaswered for some time until a naturalist by the name of Slieghet found the empty shells of two more bog turtles and turned them over to William T. Davis. Apparently these latter two specimens have received very little publicity.

The following information was taken from Mr. Davis's personal field log as recorded on May 17, 1911, by Davis himself in his

Photo by the author

*Head shot of an adult female bog turtle, Clemmys muhlenbergi. This species has a long and interesting history.*

own handwriting: "In the evening Mr. Slieghet showed me two shells of what proved to be *Chelopus muhlenbergii,* found in the nearby meadows. This was a new turtle to him." (In 1885 Schweigger placed the bog turtle in the genus *Chelopus,* but it was returned to the genus *Clemmys* sometime later.)

In 1930, C. W. Leng and W. T. Davis reported the occurrence of the bog turtle on Staten Island with some doubt. Cliford H. Pope (1946) excluded Staten Island from the range entirely; Carl F. Kauffeld (1949) also listed the bog turtle with doubt; so did Robert F. Mathewson (1955). As to whether or not Muhlenberg's turtles were indigenous to Staten Island or not, my research leads me to believe they did occur here naturally, and may have still occurred on the Island as late as 1965. In September of 1965, for instance, a man brought in to the Staten Island Zoo an adult, female bog turtle which he had found crossing a road on the south shore of Staten Island. The area he found it in was under heavy development by home builders and a road construction company. On numerous occasions I investigated the site, and found suitable habitat for bog turtles. However, it was late summer and a difficult time to find turtles because of the heavy growth of cattails, sedge grass and other vegetation growing in the swamps and bogs. I didn't see or capture another bog turtle, but did find a pair of spotted turtles, *Clemmys guttata,* in a stream which passes beneath the road where the bog turtle was found. The following spring I went back to this area only to find the habitat totally destroyed. A high school and several homes had been constructed on the site, and a new road extended through a half-mile stretch of woods causing the stream and bog to flood, forming a deep lake. Unfortunately, I wasn't able to find any additional specimens at this locality due to the destruction of the habitat. This was probably the last suitable area left on Staten Island that could support a bog turtle colony—all the others were destroyed through the years by man's encroachment on natural areas.

One of the most comprehensive papers ever published on the bog turtle was a paper by Barton and Price (1955) called "Our Knowledge of the Bog Turtle, *Clemmys muhlenbergi,* surveyed and augmented" which appeared in the scientific publication called *Copeia.* In this article the authors mentioned Staten Island specifically and quoted Ditmars' record, (1933:284-5) as follows: "Most of the writer's specimens have been caught on Staten Island, New York. They were found along marshy borders of small, clear streams." This seems further proof that the bog turtle occurred here naturally, and there is one additional record by Ditmars that Barton and Price failed to mention. This account of

Staten Island appeared in Ditmars' book entitled *The Reptile Book* (1907) in which he gives the following information: "The writer has captured several specimens on the palisades of the Hudson River and received several dozen specimens from Staten Island, New York." In view of the fact Ditmars (1907, 1933) mentions Staten Island twice in his writings as a given locality for the bog turtle, I'm in full agreement with him. Also the Barton and Price papers (1955) reflect the persuasion of Ditmars' statement.

Even though Messrs. W. T Davis (1902, 1911), C. F. Kauffeld (1949), and R. F. Mathewson (1955) all recorded the occurrence of the bog turtle on Staten Island with doubt, it doesn't necessarily prove that the turtle did not occur here naturally. It was merely their opinion, and none of the these mentioned authors were experts on bog turtles anyway. In fact, they knew only to a small degree of its habits and basic biology.

Kauffeld (1973, personal communication) never saw a bog turtle in the field or captured one, and he wasn't aware of the fact that there was a preserved bog turtle (Staten Island Museum, # 69) in the museum's collection. Kauffeld (1949) more or less based his assumption that the turtle was not found here on the following judgement: "The fact that so keen and experienced an observer as the late William T. Davis never found one is strong presumptive evidence that its natural distribution doesn't include the island." Were I to use this criteria to determine whether or not other species of "herps" occurred on Staten Island than I would have to say, for example, that the stinkpot was never found here. To convey the point, I'll cite Mathewson (1955). He reported the occurrence of the mud turtle, *Kinosternon subrubrum,* and the stinkpot, *Sternotherus odoratus,* as follows: "Few specimens are reported, but this animal is very secretive and chooses a habitat not likely to be disturbed; therefore, it is difficult to estimate local populations." If Mathewson knew anything about bog turtles he would have applied the same role to its occurrence as he did with the latter two species of turtles.

Nevertheless, I must disagree with the Mathewsons statement. I know for a fact that at the time of his writing mud turtles were fairly common on the south shore of Staten Island and, although now rare, they are still found here today. On the other hand, the stinkpot is a turtle I never caught on Staten Island. Furthermore, there is not a single preserved specimen in the Staten Island Museum's collection. So, were I to use the same criteria that Kauffeld and Mathewson used on the occurrence of the bog turtle, I would say the stinkpot should have been listed with doubt and the bog turtle as rare on Staten Island. Both the bog turtle and the stinkpot are found north, south and west of Staten Island, New York. So, geographically speaking, both turtles also occurred here, but I doubt I'll ever be able to prove, one way or the other, the occurrence of stinkpots. In any case, I think I've presented enough positive evidence that *Clemmys muhlenbergi,* was indeed part of the natural herpetological fauna of Staten Island, New York.

In 1956 the committee on herpetological common names of the American Society of Ichthyologists and Herpetologists changed the common name of *Clemmys muhlenbergi,* from Muhlenberg's turtle to the bog turtle, where it stands today.

# BOG TURTLE
*(Clemmys muhlenbergi)*

Of all the turtles known to occur in the United States, none has remained more elusive and poorly understood than the bog turtle. It is truly one of our rarest and most mysterious chelonians, and until recently information concerning this small turtle's basic biology has accumulated very slowly. This species is still common in many areas, but its habitat is seriously threatened.

### Size and Body Structure

Bog turtles are among one of the smallest species of turtles found in North America. The average adult size is about three to three and a half inches. They rarely exceed four inches; and the record size is four and a half inches (Ernst and Barbour 1972; Conant 1975).

The shape of the shell is somewhat elongated, slightly domed, with an inconspicuous keel. The carapace may or may not be rough, depending on the age of the turtle and the makeup of the substrate in which the turtle lives. Some individuals have very smooth shells with little or no annulus (growth-rings on the scutes), whereas others, even old specimens, have distinctly sculptured shells with pronounced growth rings. This variance in the epidermal scutes on the carapace is due to the strong burrowing propensities of this turtle. The marginals are smooth with the exception of the eleventh and twelfth ones, which are only slightly serrated. A well developed bridge connects the carapace with the plastron. Males have a concave plastron, long thick tails,

*n exceptionally large male bog rtle which was found in south- estern North Carolina in the ring of 1975. Note the long, ick tail and smooth shell. The rtle was marked and released its exact point of capture.*

with the anal opening extending past the margins of the carapace and larger front limbs than the females. Females have smaller slender tails that do not extend past the carapacial margins; their plastron is flat or slightly convex with a wide notch at the posterior end. Females also tend to have higher, wider carapaces.

Bog turtles' feet are poorly webbed, but are strong with sharp claws on their toes which aids them to burrow quickly into the soft, muddy bottoms of the bogs or marshes where they live.

### Coloration

The most outstanding colors on a bog turtle are the bright orange or yellow (sometimes coral-red) blotches, located on the temporal region on either side of the head. These prominent orange blotches are outstanding identifying characteristics for this species. The carapacial color may range from light to dark brown, mahogany, dark maroon or black. Some individuals may have a light brownish or orange sunburst, radiating from the center of each scute. Others may only have a few light lines on

Photo by the au

*The bog turtle is quickly d
tinguished from young wo
turtles,* Clemmys insculpta,
*the distinctive orange or yel
temporal blotches located on b
sides of the head.*

each scute or may lack markings entirely. The limbs and fleshy underparts vary from dark yellow, brownish-orange or light-red with some dark mottling. The hingeless plastron is mostly brownish-black with a light yellowish center. Between the large tympanic head blotches and around the eyes there is usually a strong marbling pattern of reddish-orange. With very old specimens the head blotches may fade or become almost completely obscured.

### Range

Plotting the range of *Clemmys muhlenbergi* is by no means an easy task. They are a victim of man's shortsighted tendency to fill in or drain bogs, marshes and grassy wetlands. This constant disturbance to their habitat, along with overcollecting, has added to the bog turtle's demise. In spite of all this the bog turtle has managed to survive in small disjunct colonies throughout portions of eastern United States. Most authorities agree that *Clemmys muhlenbergi,* occurs in at least nine of our eastern states. Its range is spotty and discontinuous as most of its colonies are separated from one another by many miles. Its main range, however, is from southwestern Massachusetts, western Connecticut and eastern New York (extinct on Staten Island), southward throughout most of New Jersey and southeastern Pennsylvania to northern Delaware and northeastern Maryland. Other populations have been discovered in southwestern Virginia, and southwestern North Carolina at elevations of over 4000 feet. There are also disjunct colonies in western New York and northwestern Pennsylvania.

### Breeding Habits

Until recently, very little was known about the courtship, mating and nesting behavior of *Clemmys muhlenbergi.* Most of the available information on this subject, as reported in the literature, dealt with captive matings and nestings under semi-natural or totally unnatural conditions. Almost nothing had been reported on their breeding habits in the wild. Throughout the course of my studies with this species, this has been one of my main concerns and the following summarizes my observations of this species in New Jersey and in southwestern North Carolina.

In New Jersey, *Clemmys muhlenbergi* usually breaks hibernation around mid-April or early May, but it varies with geographic location, and other environmental factors throughout their range. They become active when daytime air temperatures remain above 70° Fahrenheit. At this time they endeavour to climb out of the cold water onto the tops of the grass tussocks or other high and dry places, to bask in the rays of the warm spring sun. This basking behavior is very important to the bog turtles at this time because it helps them raise their body temperature properly (thermoregulation), which in turn gives them an appetite by stimulating their digestive system, and most importantly, it triggers the mating urge.

The breeding season for the bog turtle begins with the approach of warm spring days when air temperatures remain above 75° Fahrenheit. At this time the males actively search for the more secretive females, who tend to remain somewhat secluded during the early part of spring. The males travel up and down the small

streams and seepage ditches in search of a potential mate, looking everywhere possible where a female might be basking. The
mating urge seems to be foremost within the male's behavior
pattern, but should he encounter a choice food item while parading about the bog, he won't hesitate to attack and eat it.

When a male approaches another adult bog turtle, they both
usually display a series of movements which helps them determine each other's sex. In most cases, but not all, older, larger
males are the dominant turtle in such encounters. The dominant
turtle will advance towards the other turtle in a threatening
manner with its head cocked slightly to one side, displaying its
bright head-blotches. If the other turtle is a male but outside its
home-range territory within the bog, it will yield to the dominant
male by withdrawing into its shell or by fleeing rapidly from the
site without offering any resistance. However, if the turtle is
within its home-range territory he may defend it by attacking the
intruding male. The attack may be only a bluff in which the
defending turtle advances towards the intruder with mouth open
in an attempt to frighten it off, or an actual fight may ensue with
violent aggressive behavior. The biting may last anywhere from
30 seconds to 10 minutes, with each turtle trying to bite the other

Photo by Saul Fri

*The plastral view of a pair of b
turtles. The specimen on the l
is a young adult male; note t
thickness of the tail at its base a
the cloaca extends past the mo
ginal. The female on the right h
a shorter, narrower tail, and t
cloaca does not extend past t
marginal.*

*...uvenile and an old adult male turtle. The male has a con-...e plastron and very long, ...k tail.*

on the head, neck or front limbs. Once one of them has had enough and yields to the dominant turtle, it will endeavour to run away as fast as possible. The winner sometimes continues to chase after it, biting at its hind legs and tail. I have seen this aggressive behavior displayed by bog turtles both in captivity and in the wild.

When a prowling male approaches an adult female, their behavior is somewhat different. Based on my observations I believe *Clemmys muhlenbergi* has three phases to courtship and breeding behavior; these are: (1) sexual recognition; (2) aggressive biting; (3) mounting and intromission.

In the first phase the basic approach at the initial meeting has the male drawing closer to the female in a threatening manner. Sometimes the female remains perfectly still with head and limbs extended, displaying her bright head blotches, or she may withdraw slightly into her shell when the male begins his investigation. Sex recognition is achieved by visual or olfactory cues or a combination of both with the olfactory cue being the most important. Circling around her with his head fully extended, the male nudges and smells the females tail and cloacal region. He may even bite at her head and neck in an attempt to stimulate a responsive action. Courtship continues once he is sure it's a female.

Sometimes the female is not responsive and attempts to move away. The male responds by going off in another direction or by giving chase to the fleeing female.

In the second phase, if the male pursues the female, he will persistently bite her legs and head or try to get in front of her to prevent her escape. The chase may last only a few seconds or as long as half an hour or more.

On May 1, 1974, I observed a pair of bog turtles mating in the field with the aggressive phase lasting almost ten minutes. Courtship will take place in or out of the water, with the turtles showing no preference for either situation. Sometimes the female will initially be receptive; in this case the male will gently bite at her head and neck before assuming the mating position. Occasionally the male will grab hold of the fleshy skin on the female's neck and hold onto it as he positions himself on her carapace. Some females will withdraw the head and front limbs as far as they can to protect them while the aggressive male bites at the front marginals.

In most cases observed, the males in the third phase approached females from behind, climbing rapidly onto the carapace and biting at the sides of the female's head and neck, simultaneously hooking all four feet onto the edges of the marginals. If mounting took place underwater the male sometimes blew bubbles through his nostrils as he attempted to bite the female. Eventually the female would be covered properly, with the mating usually lasting anywhere from five to fifteen minutes.

I came upon a pair of mating *Clemmys muhlenbergi* in the field on May 15, 1974. The turtles were by the edge of a clump or sedge, partially covered by the overhanging blades of dried grass. The bright orange head blotches, along with some slight movement by the male caught my attention. I sat down on a tussock, took out my notebook, and quietly watched the two turtles mating. The male had all four feet hooked on the marginals of the female, but was positioned more or less to the posterior portion of her carapace, with his tail curled around the right side of hers. His front feet were stretched as far as they would go with the claws barely touching the front edge of her shell. They were joined for about six minutes from the time I discovered them, but it is not known how long they were mating before I came upon them. The female was passive, however, once released, she quickly walked away.

Although most matings take place in early spring (May), some occur as late as June. The latest I've seen bog turtles mate was June 18th. A single male may mate with several females during the course of the season. (Zappalorti 1975)

### Nesting and Egg-laying

Mid-June to early July is the primary egg-laying season for *Clemmys muhlenbergi*. This was true at least of the colony I was studying in northern New Jersey. From my observations and studies I believe most (but not all) female bog turtles nest in various grassy or mossy tussocks which grow profusely in the bogs. At this time, females must find a place in which to deposit their eggs that is above the water level and will stay relatively dry, even in the event of heavy rains. Just how they know this is poorly understood, but most females select suitable sites with good drainage.

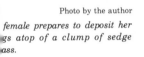

Photo by the author

*female prepares to deposit her gs atop of a clump of sedge ass.*

A gravid female will migrate to an area in the bog that has low plant growth with few or no trees. Such places are exposed to sunshine during most of the daylight hours and will provide the nest with plenty of necessary warmth during egg incubation.

Once a suitable site is selected, the female climbs up to the center and begins to construct the nest. She separates the moss or blades of dried grass with alternate movements of her hind feet. The posterior portion of her shell is gradually lowered into the depression as she digs into the soft rich topsoil (sometimes sphagnum moss) below. The depth of the nest is about one and one-half to two inches. Females usually dig as far down as their hind legs will reach. The diameter of the nest is two inches at the opening, but is somewhat larger in the chamber below where it is about two and one-half inches. Once the female is satisfied with the depth of the nest, egg-laying begins.

The average number of eggs per clutch is three eggs. Older, more mature adults may lay as many as five fertile eggs, whereas younger females will lay only one or two fertile eggs. The eggs are white and oblong, with no markings. They are about one inch long and one-half inch in diameter.

On June 13, 1974, while making some routine observations and temperature checks at one of my study bogs in northern New Jersey, I made an interesting discovery. Accompanying me were Ed Johnson and Dave Collins, two avid students of the bog turtle who were working with me as field assistants. During the course of the day we found thirteen bog turtles of various sizes along with a pair of spotted turtles. The bog turtles were checked for cloacal temperature and sex, then marked by notching their marginals. Once this information was recorded, all but one were released in the exact spot of capture. The one turtle kept was an adult female, heavy with eggs. This specimen was found in a small rivulet that flows through an open meadow within the bog, which I believe is a yearly nesting area. A second gravid female bog turtle was also found there, but she was not kept. While Dave Collins and I were investigating this part of the bog, we found an empty eggshell sticking out of the moss on top of a small tussock. The egg case appeared to be fresh, probably only a few days old. It was white with no pattern or stains. It was likely that the egg was found and eaten by a mammalian predator such as a fox, skunk or raccoon.

I began to poke around the mossy clump where the empty eggshell was found and discovered two more empty eggshells in a small depression, also covered with moss. These latter two shells were badly discolored and stained from age, which meant they were quite old, probably last year's eggs. The shells and egg chamber were measured and photographed. Then the empty egg cases were removed and taken for preservation in the Staten Island Zoo's preserve collection as proof of our find. As I went to

Photo by the author

*ward Johnson, my research*
*ociate, takes the cloacal temper-*
*re of an adult female bog turtle.*

cover up the depression, I started to poke my fingers gently into the grass and moss. Much to my surprise I felt something hard. Quickly spreading the moss aside, I found three more eggs. This nest chamber was only five inches away from the other nest.

These three eggs were intact and appeared to have been recently laid. The eggs and nest chamber were measured and photographed, then carefully removed to a container and taken back to the Staten Island Zoo for incubation. I chose not to leave the eggs in the field for fear of predators returning to eat them.

The eggs were placed in a two and one-half gallon glass aquarium on a bed of spagnum moss three inches deep. Then they were covered with two more inches of sphagnum. During incubation the eggs were kept at a temperature of 75° F at night and 85° F. during the day. On July 28th, 1974, all three eggs hatched exactly forty-six days after they were found. The gravid female taken on the same day the eggs were found (June 13, 1974) laid three eggs on June 19, 1974, in a nest of sphagnum moss. These were set up in a separate glass aquarium at the same temperature as the other three eggs. The average measurement of the six eggs was one and one-eighth inches in length, by three-fourths of an inch in width. These hatched on August 1, 1974, a total of forty-five days from the time of deposition. Because both aquaria containing the eggs were kept under the same temperature and conditions as the first clutch found in the field, I believe the first batch was laid only one or two days before we found it.

On the morning of July 28th, 1974, I witnessed the hatching of two of the eggs; a third egg case was already empty. The turtle

Photo by the aut

*Taking measurements of a n which contains 3 good eggs* Clemmys muhlenbergi.

*bog turtle emerging from its
egg; the caruncle is quite noticeable on tip of its snout.*

had emerged during the night and burrowed down into the sphagnum moss. I noticed slits in both of the remaining eggs. Soon afterwards a small head popped out of one of them, bearing the unmistakable bright head blotches. The turtle remained inside the egg for three hours with only its head protruding from the shell. This was probably to clear its lungs of any mucus and to use up as much of the yolk as possible before emergence. Eventually it crawled out of the shell and immediately burrowed into the sphagnum moss. Upon inspection of the hatchling I noticed a small yolk-sac still attached to the center of the plastron (one-quarter of an inch in diameter). This was completely absorbed in forty-eight hours. A prominent caruncle (egg-toothlike modification of the skin), was present on the tip of the snout, just below the nostrils. This also disappeared in several days. When the turtles

first emerged from the egg, their shells were extremely elongated, almost the exact shape of the eggshell itself, but they flattened somewhat within one day. One of the hatchlings measured one and one-quarter inches in length and three-quarters of an inch in width. In two days the length did not change, but the width now measured three-fourths of an inch. While the yolk-sac was being absorbed and for several days afterwards, the baby bog turtles remained burrowed under damp sphagnum moss and did not feed.

Their carapace was dark brown with some slight black flecks scattered irregularly about. The plastron had a dark center figure with a light yellow border. The limbs and tail were brown with some dark orange markings, and the temporal head blotches were large and bright yellowish-orange in color.

Because of their secretive habits and strong burrowing propensities, it is almost impossible to study the habits and behavior of juvenile bog turtles in the wild. However, observations under semi-natural conditions have shown that they are extremely secretive during parts of the day, but come out regularly to bask and feed just as the adults do. They seem to show a tendency to be

The yolk-sac or "button" is st
evident on the center of t
plastron.

somewhat more aquatic than the adults and to remain in seclusion during the hot weather.

### Adult Behavior

After the breeding season is over and egg-laying has taken place, both the males and females return to their home-range territory within the bog. Basking and foraging for food becomes their main activity during the rest of the year.

Bog turtles emerge from their muddy burrows when air temperatures are above seventy degrees F. Basking takes place either in or out of the water. Sometimes the turtles will climb up on a clump of sedge grass in order to thermoregulate. Once the

*is hatchling, not much larger
m a penny, was found by the
thor in a sphagnum bog in
uthwestern North Carolina.*

proper amount of sunlight has been absorbed, the turtle will then endeavor to forage for food.

### Diet

They are most aggressive predators when searching for food. In the field I have seen bog turtles feed on the following: wood frogs, bullfrogs, and its tadpoles, field crickets, slugs, snails, nestling birds and crayfish.

In captivity I have fed bog turtles the following food items: chopped beef heart, chopped horse meat, chopped shrimp, small mice (live), earthworms (live), meal worms (live), crickets (live), cockroaches (live), snails (live), slugs (live).

Photo by the auth
*Slugs are among one of the ma*
*food items of* Clemmys muhle
bergi.

Live food always stimulated the turtles into feeding, and even picky feeders could be induced to eat when offered a live insect or small mouse. They were occasionally fed some fruits and vegetables, but they seemed to show a preference for live prey. Some of the plants I've seen bog turtles feed on in the wild are the tender young shoots of the skunk cabbage, and leaves and stems of watercress.

Barton and Price (1955) report the presence of seeds in the stomachs of bog turtles which they examined. These were the

Photo by the author
*s brightly marked female is tly foraging for food.*

seeds of pond weed (Potamogeton) and large amounts of seeds of a sedge grass (carex).

*Clemmys muhlenbergi* is an omnivorous feeder and can eat in or out of water, showing no apparent preference for either situation. They are opportunistic feeders and will eat the food items available to them as they are encountered in the bog.

Ernst and Barbour (1972) report they have never seen *Clemmys muhlenbergi* active earlier than 11:00 a.m. or later than 4:00 p.m. Dave Collins, a fellow student of the bog turtle who carried out field observations for two years in the bogs of Pennsylvania, informed me that he has seen *Clemmys muhlenbergi* basking at the edge of rivulets as early as 7:00 a.m. in the morning on a number of occasions. Another fellow student, Dick Holub, who lives in northern New Jersey, has made similar observations

with the populations in his area. Dick has seen bog turtles active
and basking on sunny mornings at 8:00 a.m. and as late as 6:00
p.m. in the afternoon. My observations support both of these
workers. I too have seen bog turtles basking on sedge grass or in
shallow, muddy water at all times during the day. It should be
mentioned, however, that most of these observations were made
during the months of June and July. During August and early
September the turtle is much harder to find.

Bog turtles are active during any time of the day, provided the
air temperature is at least 65° F. Basking is the primary activity
from the time when they emerge from their muddy burrow until
their body temperature us raised sufficiently to allow foraging for
food. Most of the specimens I examined while basking had cloacal
temperatures of 60° F to 74° F, whereas the turtles that were

Photo by the aut

*A pair of juvenile bog turtles t*
*were marked by notching i*
*marginals with a file. Afterwa*
*they were released at the ex*
*point of capture.*

parading around the bog or foraging for food had cloacal temperatures of 74° F to 80°F. When daytime temperatures become too hot (over 85° F), the bog turtles are somewhat inactive, especially the juveniles. During extremely hot weather they probably estivate in their burrows.

### General Discussion

The bog turtle is a victim of man's shortsighted tendency to fill in or drain bogs, marshes and grassy wetlands. If it is to be saved from extinction, its habitat must first be protected and set aside with the protection of state and federal agencies. Effective legislation must also be passed and enforced to further protect this shy little turtle. Both the Internationl Union for the Conservation of Nature and Natural Resources and the United States Department of the Interior have placed *Clemmys muhlenbergi* on their rare and endangered species lists.

Laws alone cannot save the bog turtle; the remaining populations in the wild and their habitats must be left undisturbed by land developers, commercial pet dealers, and private collectors. Effective conservation efforts are essential to the survival of this turtle. A greater awareness of our part is also necessary for the protection of all wildlife in general and the elusive bog turtle in particular. If we save the bog turtle's marshy habitats, we shall save the turtle, it's as simple as that.

## BOX TURTLES (Genus *Terrapene*)

These are wide-ranging, terrestrial turtles with high-domed, elongated carapaces. Their bilobed plastron is equipped with the box turtle's most conspicuous characteristics—a hinge which allows the turtle to close its shell completely. This is one of the few turtles in the world with such a tight-fitting hinged plastron. With some individuals the shell closes so tightly that no trace of the head, tail or limbs can be seen.

The genus is exclusively North American, ranging over a wide portion of the eastern and central United States, down throughout most of Mexico. In the eastern part of the country there are four subspecies. These are:

A.  Eastern Box Turtle, *Terrapene carolina carolina*
B.  Gulf Coast Box Turtle, *Terrapene carolina major*
C.  Three-Toed Box Turtle, *Terrapene carolina triunguis*
D.  Florida Box Turtle, *Terrapene carolina bauri*

The Ornate Box Turtle occurs in central United States. There are two subspecies.

    A.  Ornate Box Turtle, *Terrapene ornata ornata*
    B.  Desert Box Turtle, *Terrapene ornata luteola*

The member of the genus most familiar to me is the eastern box turtle. As a representative of this group, a brief account of its description and habits is given next.

## EASTERN BOX TURTLE
### (Terrapene carolina carolina)

This turtle usually has a high dome-shaped shell and demonstrates a wide array of colors and patterns on the carapace and plastron from one individual to the next. They are often picked up in fields and wooded areas or found crossing roadways. They make good pets and adapt well to captivity.

Photo by the aut

*An ornate box turtle* Terrap ornata ornata *withdraws to safety of its shell.*

*The yellow bellied turtle,* Chrysemys scripts scripts, *is a common species throughout the coastal plain of the eastern United States from southeastern Virginia to northern Florida.*

*This hatchling red-eared turtle,* Chrysemys scripta elegans, *an albino with pink eyes, is in the collection of the Philadelphia Zoo. It was acquired by the zoo from an animal dealer.*

*A normally colored adult red-eared turtle with the typical elongated reddish marking extending from behind the eye.*

Photo by the author
*A yearling red-bellied turtle,* Chrysemys rubriventris rubriventris, *foraging for food among aquatic vegetation.*

Photo by the author
*The eastern chicken turtle,* Dierochelys reticularia reticularia, *is usually very shy when first captured and may remain inside its shell making identification difficult. Look for a net-like pattern on the carapace and bold vertical yellow stripes on the hind legs.*

Photo by Saul Friess
*Blanding's turtle* Emydoidea blandingi, *is sometimes referred to as the "semi-box turtle" because of the presence of a single hinge across the plastron. Like the chicken turtle, they have long necks.*

*The gopher tortoise,* Gopherus polyphemus, *is the only true tortoise found in the eastern states. They have high-domed shells and elephant-like feet.*

*The Atlantic hawksbill,* Eretmochelys imbricata imbricata, *has been hunted relentlessly as a source of food as well as for their carapace which is used to make various commercial items out of it such as tortoise shell combs, buttons, jewelry etc. Notice the beak-like jaws, the reason for its name.*

*Gopher tortoises live in deep burrows throughout their entire lives. The burrow offers them shelter and protection from their enemies, although many other animals often share the holes with the tortoise.*

*The eastern spiny softshell turtle,* Trionyx spiniferus spiniferus, *is basically a river turtle, but it occurs in muddy or sandy bottomed ponds and lakes as well. It ranges over a large area of the Mississippi Valley to the Gulf and north to western New York state. It has been introduced into the Pine Barrens in southern New Jersey.*

*The snorkel-like nostrils of the softshell turtle is a special adaptation which allows the turtle to take air into its lungs exposing nothing more than the tubular nostrils above the surface of the water.*

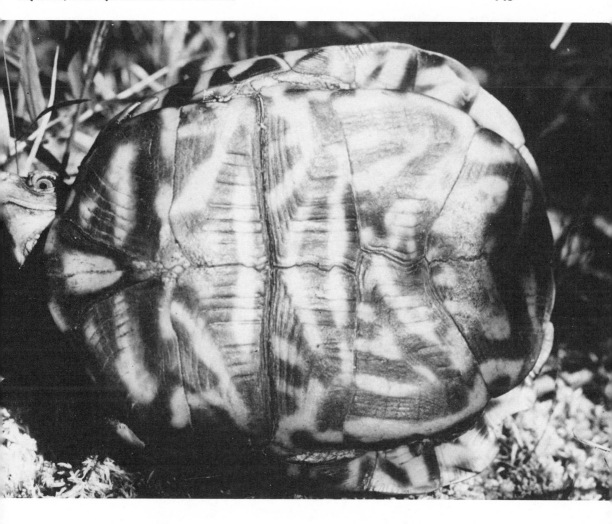

Photo by the author

*ttom view of an ornate box
showing the well developed
e. Males have a concave
on.*

## Size and Body Structure

The average adult size is from four and one-half to six inches.
Conant (1958) gives a record size of six and one-half inches, but
since the publication of his book, larger specimens have been
recorded. Cook, Abb, and Frair (1972) reported a record-breaking
individual that measured seven and thirteen-sixteenths inches.

The high shell is round dorsally and somewhat elongated with
a prominent vertebral keel. Their plastron is connected by a
poorly developed bridge, but has a well-developed hinge between
the pectoral and abdominal shields. Although there are no major
sexual differences in *Terrapene carolina carolina,* some minor
sexual dimorphism does exist which aids in determining sex.

Males usually have:
1. A concave, posterior plastral lobe
2. Hind claws that are thick, curved and long
3. Long, thick tails

Females usually have:
1. A flat or slightly convex posterior plastral lobe
2. Hind claws that are thinner and straighter
3. Short, thin tails

*Coloration*

The carapacial colors and patterns of *Terrapene carolina carolina* are extremely variable. In most cases it is usually some shade of brown with yellow, orange, olive or red. These may be broken up with black radiating lines, spots, blotches or bars on each shield. The plastron may have dark patches and spots bordered with yellow or be completely black or brown. The head and limbs as well as the soft fleshy parts are brownish-yellow or orange with streaks or spots.

In most cases, but not all, males have red eyes, whereas females

Photo by the ‹
*The Florida box turtle, Terra‹ carolina bauri, is found thr‹ out most of Florida.*

*e: An adult male eastern box
. They are often present near
ms or bogs, and are easily
l after summer rains.*

*t: An aggressive male east-
box turtle endeavors to mate
a shy female. I once observed
ale continually courting a
le for over 5 hours until mat-
ook place.*

tend to have brown or yellow eyes. But eye coloration is not a good means of distinguishing sex because I have seen males with brown eyes and females with red eyes.

### Range

The eastern box turtle occurs from southern Maine to Georgia in the east and west to Michigan, Illinois and Tennessee. It is known to intergrade with all other three subspecies where the ranges overlap. It is still common on parts of Long Island and Staten Island, New York.

## DIAMONDBACK TERRAPINS (Genus *Malaclemys)*

Diamondback terrapins are truly our only salt-marsh turtles with the same structural characteristics as the freshwater turtles (they do not have flippers like the true sea turtles of the families Cheloniidae and Dermochelyidae). Rarely do they stray from coastal salt or brackish waters.

At one time diamondback terrapins were popular as a gourmet's dish. A delicious stew or soup can be made from their flesh. This turtle was hunted in such great numbers that the population became dangerously low in many areas. However, in recent years people seem to have lost their taste for terrapin stew and the species has made a fantastic comeback in many coastal marshes where it once was rare.

The genus *Malaclemys* includes a single species, of which there are seven races recognized. The seven subspecies range continuously along our coastal waters from New England (Cape Cod), southward to Florida and the Keys, and along the Gulf Coast to western Texas and possibly into Mexican coastal waters. Because the ranges of the various subspecies of *Malaclemys* overlap so much, a great deal of intergradation takes place making identification of some of the races very difficult.

The diamondback terrapins—the seven races of *Malaclemys* are:

    A. Northern Diamondback Terrapin, *Malaclemys terrapin terrapin*

    B. Carolina Diamondback Terrapin, *Malaclemys terrapin centrata*

    C. Florida East Coast Terrapin, *Malaclemys terrapin tequesta*

    D. Mangrove Terrapin, *Malaclemys terrapin rhizophorarum*

    E.  Ornate Diamondback Terrapin, *Malaclemys terrapin macrospilota*

    F.  Mississippi Diamondback Terrapin, *Malaclemys terrapin pileata*

    G.  Texas Diamondback Terrapin, *Malaclemys terrapin littoralis*

The only member of this genus that occurs in the coastal waters of New York and New Jersey is the northern diamondback terrapin. I have collected adults and juveniles in the wild on many occasions and have observed the nesting behavior of females in spring.

# NORTHERN DIAMONDBACK TERRAPIN
## (Malaclemys terrapin terrapin)

This turtle's most outstanding characteristic is the bold concentric markings and grooves on each large carapacial shield. Thus, the reason for the name, diamondback terrapin.

### *Size and Body Structure*

Females of this genus grow considerably larger than males. An average-male is about four to five inches, with the record size being five and one-half inches. With females the average size is six to seven and one-half inches; the largest recorded female measured eight and one-half inches.

These are small to medium-sized turtles with extremely sculptured shells. The head, neck, limbs and fleshy underparts are usually heavily marked with dark flecks or spots. A vertebral keel is present on the center of the oblong carapace. The posterior marginals are sometimes slightly curled up and the shell is widest just behind the well-developed bridge. Their plastron is smooth and flat and the limbs are powerful with strong webbing on each foot.

### *Coloration*

The carapace varies from black, brown or some shade of gray. Their flat plastron is usually gray, olive-green, orange or yellow and sometimes marked with dark irregular spots or blotches. The limbs, fleshy underparts and head are lightly flecked with white

or light gray markings on a ground color of black or gray. With both sexes the eyes are usually black. A typical *Malaclemys terrapin terrapin* often has a dark mustache like marking along the upper jaw.

### Range

The northern diamondback terrapin occurs along our Atlantic coastal waters and estuaries from Cape Cod, southward to Cape

Photo by Tony D

*At one time diamondba*
*rapins were hunted comme*
*because the turtles were a p*
*gourmet dish; as a result the*
*lations became dangerous*
*Nowdays people seem to ha*
*their taste for them and the*
*made a strong comeback ir*
*where they once were rare.*

Hatteras where it intergrades with the Carolina diamondback terrapin, *Malaclemys terrapin centrata*.

### General Discussion

Because this turtle had a high economic value as a food source for man at one time, much research and breeding was carried out. Most of this turtle's habits and behavior have been well documented in the literature (See Ernst and Barbour 1972, Carr 1952, etc). For this reason its further discussion here seems unwarranted.

### MAP TURTLES AND SAWBACKS (Genus *Graptemys*)

These turtles received their common or vernacular name "map turtles" because most members of the genus are adorned with beautiful, bright map-like patterns and colors on their carapace, whereas others of this genus have high carapacial dorsal keels, or knobby, upward projections, thus winning them the name "sawbacks."

Members of the genus *Graptemys* are primarily turtles of our

Photo by Saul Friess

*chling northern diamond-*
*errapin. These small turtles*
*ey to seagulls, ghost crabs,*
*fish and a host of other*
*tors.*

larger bodies of fresh water and rivers. There are ten species found in the eastern half of the United States. Some have a limited distribution and are restricted to a single river system. Map turtles demonstrate considerable sexual dimorphism, both in adult size and coloration. Hatchlings have the brightest colors and knobby projections on their shells and most of these characteristics are retained, to some degree, by the smaller-sized adult males. By contrast, the mature females tend to lose most of the juvenile pattern and coloration on the carapace. Adult females also grow twice the size of the males. The size of the average female ranges from seven to eleven and one-half inches. The smaller males average from four to six and one-half inches.

For a comprehensive account of the life histories of the various species of *Graptemys*, the reader is referred to Ernst and Barbour (1972).

The ten species of *Graptemys* that occur in the United States are:

　　1. Map Turtle, *Graptemys geographica*

Photo by the a...

*A portrait of a Mississippi turtle,* Graptemys kohni, *s... ing the distinct, crescent-sh... yellow marking behind its si... colored eye. Like most map tu... this species is highly aquatic can be found in most unpopul... rivers, canals and waterway... eastern United States.*

2. Barbour's Map Turtle, *Graptemys barbouri*
3. Alabama Map Turtle, *Graptemys pulchra*
4. Mississippi Map Turtle, *Graptemys kohni*
5. The False Map Turtles; three subspecies are recognized:
   A. False Map Turtle,
      *Graptemys pseudogeographica pseudogeographica*
   B. Ouachita Map Turtles,
      *Graptemys pseudogeographica ouachitensis*
   C. Sabine Map Turtle,
      *Graptemys pseudogeographica sabinensis*
6. Texas Map Turtle, *Graptemys versa*
7. Cagle's Map Turtle, *Graptemys caglei*
8. Ringed Sawback, *Graptemys oculifera*
9. Yellow-Blotched Sawback, *Graptemys flavimaculata*
10. The Black-Knobbed Sawbacks; two subspecies are recognized:

Photo by Jack Muntzner

*his strange looking false map rtle, Graptemys pseudogeo-aphica, was in the collection of e Staten Island Zoo. It lived al-st 1½ years and was quite an traction to our zoo visitors. Both ads could eat and sometimes uld fight over their food. The rtle eventually died of natural uses and is now in our preserved llection.*

    A.  Black-Knobbed Sawback,
        *Graptemys nigrinoda nigrinoda*
    B.  Delta Black-Knobbed Sawback,
        *Graptemys nigrinoda delticola*

## PAINTED TURTLES AND THEIR RELATIVES
### (Genus *Chrysemys*)

This is a large genus with some fifteen known species ranging from southern Canada to southern Brazil. The genus is also known from some of the islands in the West Indies.

Originally most of the species within this group were in the genus *Pseudemys*, but McDowell (1964) revised *Chrysemys* to include all of the members of *Pseudemys*. Zug (1966) did a study of the penial morphology of the *Pseudemys-Chrysemys* complex and Weaver and Rose (1967) carried out osteologic studies of both genera. These works supported the conclusion of McDowell (1964). Ernst and Barbour (1972) also recognize the reclassification and so does Conant (1975).

Included in the genus *Chrysemys* are most of the larger-sized basking turtles that live in permanent bodies of fresh water throughout the eastern and central parts of the United States. Most members have smooth, unkeeled shells, and bright colors and patterns. They are medium to large-sized turtles and are called by such odd names as Cooters, Sliders and Red-Bellies. There are seven U.S. species within the genus; these are:

1. The Painted Turtles; four subspecies are recognized:
    A.  Eastern Painted Turtle,
        *Chrysemys picta picta*
    B.  Midland Painted Turtle,
        *Chrysemys picta marginata*
    C.  Souther Painted Turtle,
        *Chrysemys picta dorsalis*
    D.  Western Painted Turtle,
        *Chrysemys picta belli*

2. The Pond Sliders; four subspecies have been described:
    A.  Yellow-Bellied turtle,
        *Chrysemys scripta scripta*
    B.  Red-Eared Turtle,
        *Chrysemys scripta elegans*
    C.  Cumberland Turtle,
        *Chrysemys scripta troosti*
    D.  Big Bend Turtle,
        *Chrysemys scripta gaigeae*

*An adult female red-eared turtle,* Chrysemys scripta elegans, *basking on a log. This is the species that was exploted in five and dime stores for many years. They are now protected by strong laws which restrict their sale.*

3. The River Cooters, five subspecies occur in the United States:

   A. River Cooter,
      *Chrysemys concinna concinna*

   B. Suwanee Cooter,
      *Chrysemys concinna suwanniensis*

   C. Mobile Cooter,
      *Chrysemys concinna mobilensis*

   D. Slider,
      *Chrysemys concinna hieroglyphica*

   E. Texas Slider,
      *Chrysemys concinna texana*

4. The Peninsula Cooters; three subspecies are known:

   A. Florida Cooter,
      *Chrysemys floridana floridana*

*Above: A large river coote.
Chrysemys concinna concinn*
*soaking up the sun on a cora*
*bank. This is a common turtle*
*the southeastern United States.*

*Left: Most of the canals and lake*
*in northern Florida have thei*
*share of the Florida coote*
Chrysemys floridana floridan*
*They range northward along th*
*coastal plain to Virginia.*

B.  Peninsula Cooter,
    *Chrysemys floridana peninsularis*
C.  Missouri Slider,
    *Chrysemys floridana hoyi*
5. The Red-Bellied Turtles; two subspecies have been described:
A.  Red-Bellied Turtle,
    *Chrysemys rubriventris rubriventris*
B.  Plymouth Turtle,
    *Chrysemys rubriventris bangsi*
6. Florida Red-Bellied Turtle,
   *Chrysemys nelsoni*
7. Alabama Red-Bellied Turtle,
   *Chrysemys alabamensis*

Photo by the author

*A small red-bellied turtle, Chrysemys rubriventris rubriventris, feeding on a luckless earthworm on the bottom of the pond.*

The subspecies I am most familiar with in this genus is the eastern painted turtle, it being one of the first kinds of turtles I collected and kept as a pet and a form which I have studied over the years.

# EASTERN PAINTED TURTLE
### (Chrysemys picta picta)

The most outstanding characteristic of the eastern painted turtle is the alignment of the costal and vertebral seams on the carapace. These large shields approach straight rows across the shell. In all other North American turtles and possibly all in the world, the shields down the center of the carapace alternate with the two outer rows. The seams between the shields are bordered with light orange, brown or red.

### Size and Body Structure

Similar to the other members of this genus, the females grow larger than the males. Length of the average male is about four and one-half inches. Some may reach five and one-half inches; whereas the average size for females is about six inches. The largest female on record measured seven and one-eighth inches (Conant 1975).

The carapace is keelless, oval-shaped, somewhat flattened and very smooth. The flat, hingeless plastron is connected to the upper shell by a well-developed bridge. The marginals are smooth and lack serrations with the exception of the nuchal and first marginals behind the head. These are slightly serrated. The upper jaw is strongly notched. The smaller-sized adult males have long foreclaws and long, thick tails with their vent (cloacal opening) extending past the edge of the carapace. Females have short foreclaws and higher, domed shells and short tails. Their vent does not extend past the marginals.

### Coloration

Just as their name implies, these are colorful turtles. The carapace is usually dark brown, olive or black with the marginals

Photo by the author

*t the name implies, the eastern*
*inted turtle is adorned with*
*tremely bright colors. The*
*astron is usually orange or*
*llow and some individuals may*
*ave a dark center figure. The*
*ndersides of the marginals are*
*right red and black.*

heavily pigmented with bright red (sometimes orange or yellow), half-circles and lines that extend underneath the sides and onto the bridge.

The plastron may be yellow, orange or cream-colored with a dark center figure on some individuals. The fleshy underparts, neck and limbs are adorned with bright red lines on a black ground-color. A series of bright yellow lines are present on the face, head and neck. The eyes are black and yellow. Sometimes the upper and lower shells may become coated or encrusted with a brownish-red deposit from the water in which they live, thus hiding their true colors.

### Range

*Chrysemys picta picta* ranges from southeastern Canada (Nova Scotia) through New England and the Atlantic coastal plains to Georgia and westward to eastern Alabama. A great amount of intergradation often takes place between the subspecies wherever their respective ranges overlap.

### Breeding Habits

In most cases, males reach sexual maturity in their fifth year. Most females are sexually mature and ready for egg-laying in their sixth year, but this varies with geographic location and other factors. On Staten Island, New York, courtship and mating begins in early April and extends into late May or early June.

Photo by Manuel R....

*A gravid female eastern pain... turtle in the process of layi... eggs. The nest is constructed w... alternate movements of the h... feet, her eggs will hatch in ab... 75 days.*

Courtship usually takes place in open, shallow water at a depth of one or two feet. Males will court females as they are encountered or they may occasionally seek them out during peak breeding season. Sexual recognition is achieved by visual and olfactory cues.

Once a male encounters a potential mate, courtship begins. He will swim up to the female and try to position himself in front of her, head-on, face to face. Using his long foreclaws, he gently strokes and waves at the female's face and head. This stroking behavior is an important stimulus to the female and triggers her mating urge. If the female is receptive, she will stroke the male's front feet with her foreclaws. He will then endeavor to stimulate the female to follow him to the bottom. Once she is resting on the bottom, the male then swims on top, mounts her from behind by hooking his claws on the edges of her shell, and wraps his tail beneath hers. Mating lasts anywhere from three to fifteen minutes. On May 15, 1969 I watched a pair of *Chrysemys picta picta* mate for ten minutes in a shallow pond on Staten Island. About a half hour later I saw the same male court another female and succeeded in mating with her also.

### Egg-laying

Gravid females begin to deposit their eggs around early June, but the peak of the nesting activity is mid-June to early July. Early morning or late afternoon is when females usually lay their eggs. I have seen painted turtles digging nest chambers as early as 7:00 a.m. and as late at night as 8:30 p.m. The nest usually is constructed in soft, loamy soil or sandy soil with good drainage. High banks or hillsides near ponds and lakes or soft roadside shoulders are common nesting sites. Females dig the nest with alternate movements of their hind feet. The nest is somewhat flask shaped, being wider at the bottom. The mouth of the nest is about two inches in diameter and the depth is usually three and one-half inches. Most females lay three to eight elliptical white eggs. Larger females may deposit as many as ten or eleven eggs. The eggs measure one and one-eight to one and three-eights of an inch in length and are about one-half inch in diameter. The incubation period is about seventy-five days, but it varies with temperature and other environmental conditions. The average-sized hatchling painted turtle is about one and one-eighth inches long and somewhat round in shape. Young *Chrysemys picta picta* are far more colorful than the adults. They grow fast and almost double their size in one year.

### Adult Behavior

Eastern painted turtles are avid sun-worshippers and sometimes spend several hours a day in the sun on their favorite basking site. Most *Chrysemys picta picta* use the same rock, log or bank for daily basking, whenever temperature and weather conditions are favorable. Sometimes basking sites are shared with several individuals of the same species or with other species of turtles as well.

Once their body temperature has been raised sufficiently (about 78° to 82° F) by basking, foraging for food begins. Painted turtles are omnivorous feeders; they eat most species of aquatic plants and animals with which they share the habitat. Hatchling and young *Chrysemys* tend to be more carnivourous in their feeding habits, but become herbivorous as they mature.

Painted turtles remain somewhat active during cold weather and will even bask on warm winter days. I once saw over two dozen individuals moving about under the ice of a frozen lake. The turtles were moving lethargically along the bottom in various directions without any apparent purpose. Several of these specimens were easily captured after I chopped through the ice. This is a good example of how some aquatic species of turtles augment their respiratory needs by using the lining of the mouth cavity as sort of a gill. Water is brought in and out of the nasal openings and dissolved oxygen is extracted from the water by the highly vascular pharyngeal passage of the mouth and throat region.

## THE CHICKEN TURTLES (Genus *Deirochelys*)

Chicken turtles may be easily distinguished from other similar species by looking at the rump and tail region. They have a characteristic pattern of vertical stripes on the hind legs. Both forelegs have broad yellow strips. Other characteristics to look for are an extremely long neck and a netlike pattern on the carapace.

This is a small genus with a single species of which three subspecies are recognized. These are:
1. The Chicken Turtles:
   A. Eastern Chicken Turtle,
      *Dierochelys reticularia reticularia*
   B. Florida Chicken Turtle,
      *Dierochelys reticularia chrysea*
   C. Western Chicken Turtle,
      *Dierochelys reticularia miaria*

# EASTERN CHICKEN TURTLE

*(Dierochelys reticularia reticularia)*

### Size and Body Structure

These are small to medium-sized turtles. The average size is four to six inches, but specimens up to ten inches have been recorded. Females grow larger than males.

The long carapace is smooth and covered with a strong netlike pattern, but this may be covered with a thick growth of algae. The neck is extra long; when it is stretched all the way out it is almost as long as the plastron. The unkeeled carapace is connected to the flat plastron by a well-developed bridge. Adult males have long foreclaws and long thick tails. Females have higher, more domed shells.

Photo by the author

*adult female eastern chicken* *tle,* Dierochelys reticularia *icularia, basking on a log. tice the long neck and netlike ttern on the carapace.*

## Coloration

The reticulate netlike-pattern of the carapace is yellow or orange on a ground color of olive, tan or light brown. They have light yellow, sometimes orange, plastrons with no markings. As mentioned, look for the "striped pants" on the rump and the wide yellow stripe on the forelimbs. Yellow stripes are also present on the face, neck and limbs.

Photo by Saul Fri[...]

*The author photographing a y[...]*
*low-bellied turtle and an easte[...]*
*chicken turtle basking on a l[...]*
*A camera is the best tool for c[...]*
*lecting herptiles.*

*bove: This is the picture taken*
*y the author.*

Photo by the author

*ight: A long stretch—an eastern*
*icken turtle showing the length*
*its neck.*

## *Range*

The Eastern chicken turtle is found along the Atlantic and Gulf coastal plains from southeastern Virginia to the Mississippi River. They inhabit still waters of large lakes and marshes or roadside ditches and ponds. They occasionally travel overland in search of better feeding grounds or higher waters. The basking behavior is well developed in this species, and I have frequently seen them sunning on logs and stumps in southern South Carolina.

## BLANDING'S TURTLE (Genus *Emydoidea*)

These turtles easily are recognized because they have a well-developed hinged plastron and an extremely long neck which is bright yellow underneath. The genus has but a single species with no subspecies recognized. They are restricted to extreme southern Canada and northern United States.

They often are referred to as the semi-box turtle because of their hinged plastron. Surprisingly enough, little is known about the behavior and breeding habits of this large turtle. Their nesting in the wild has been observed only a few times. Gibbons (1968) observed nesting in June, but little information has been gathered on their breeding activity other than that. This is an attractive and interesting turtle which should be investigated further to determine the current status of populations within its discontinuous range.

# THE BLANDING'S TURTLE
*(Emydoidea blandingi)*

These are large aquatic turtles with long necks and notched upper jaw. There is little sexual dimorphism with *Emydoidea blandingi*. Both sexes average about the same size and coloration. Males have slightly thicker and longer tails with the cloacal opening located behind the edge of the carapace. Their plastron is somewhat concave, but not as deep as on the box turtles.

## *Size and Body Structure*

The average-sized Blanding's turtle is from five to seven and one-half inches, but specimens up to ten and one-half inches have been recorded (Conant 1975).

Photo by Saul Friess

*The Blanding's turtle,* Emydoidea *blandingi, is a large aquatic species with a single belly hinge which allows the turtle to close the shell almost as tightly as a box turtle.*

The carapace is elongated, unkeeled and smooth, but is slightly domed. They have flat plastrons with a strong, functional hinge between the pectoral and abdominal shields. Their head is large and flat with bulging eyes.

### Coloration

Blanding's turtles generally have a blue-black coloration on the carapace and part of the plastron, but this is covered with numerous light yellow or tan spots which tend to run together in the shape of streaks or bars. The upper portion of the mouth, chin and throat are bright yellow and the eyes black with yellow or orange borders.

## Range

*Emydoidea blandingi* occurs from southern Ontario southward to the region of the Great Lakes and western to eastern Nebraska. It has a discontinuous range with populations in Massachusetts, southern New Hampshire, Nova Scotia, and eastern New York. Although this turtle is still common in some parts of its range, it is now quite rare in other areas where it once was common.

# Chapter 7

# DESERT AND GOPHER TORTOISES

This is a large and diverse family with representatives occuring in Africa, Europe, Asia, North America, South America, Mexico and on several ocean islands. The family is composed of ten genera and some 39 known living species of tortoises.

Contained in the family *Testudinidae* are the largest living land turtles known to science. Including such giants as the Galapagos tortoise, *Geochelone elephantopus* of the Galapagos Islands off the coast of Ecuador, and the Aldabra tortoise, *Geochelone gigantea* of the Seychelles Islands. Throughout the world tortoises have adapted well to a variety of different habitats. The desert tortoise, *Gopherus agassizi*, lives in the hot, dry deserts of the American Southwest, and in almost complete contrast, the red-footed tortoise, *Geochelone carbonaria,* makes its home in the tropical rain forest of northern South America. The pancake tortoise, *Malacochersus tonieri,* is a highly specialized form from Kenya and Tanzania, Africa. This tortoise is characterized by an extremely flat carapace, thus the reason for its common name, and it also has a soft, flexible shell. They can move faster than other tortoises and when they sense danger they seek shelter in the crevices in rocks and have the ability to wedge themselves in so tightly that the tortoise cannot be dislodged.

The United States has a single genus—*Gopherus*—of which there are three distinct species. These are:

1. Desert Tortoise, *Gopherus agassizi*
2. Texas Tortoise, *Gopherus berlandieri*
3. Gopher Tortoise, *Gopherus polyphemus*

## GOPHER TORTOISE
### (*Gopherus polyphemus*)

Of these three species, the one I have had the best opportunity to study in the field is the gopher tortoise. A description of some of its habits in the wild as well as its identifying characteristics follows.

These are large, totally terrestrial turtles whose range is restricted to the southeastern portion of the United States. The most outstanding identifying characteristic of the gopher tortoise is the elongated gular projection of the plastron, small elephantine hind limbs, and large shovel-like front limbs.

Photo by Saul Fri[e]

*An adult male gopher turt[le] emerging from its burrow to beg[in] its daily activity of foraging f[or] food.*

### Size and Body Structure

The average size is six to nine and a half inches. The record size is fourteen and a half inches. The carapace is sort of helmet-shaped, lacks a keel and is highest in the sacral region. There are pronounced growth rings on both the carapace and the plastron and the marginals are smooth with the exception of the six posterior ones which are slightly serrated. A large gular projection extends from the anterior portion of the lower shell and a well-developed bridge connects the upper shell to the hingeless, flat plastron. They have large, rounded heads with jaws that are somewhat serrated. The hind limbs are short and stumpy, whereas the front legs are large, flat and shovel-like in shape. The front claws are sharp, flat and rounded on the ends.

### Coloration

The high shell is usually some shade of brown, gray or sometimes black. Younger individuals often have light yellowish or orange centers on each large shield on the carapce. The plastron is light brown or yellow. The head, neck, limbs and fleshy underparts are grayish-black. The eyes are dark brown. Older specimens sometimes have smoother shells than young individuals, a result of burrowing in sandy soil.

### Range

The gopher tortoise occurs along the sand hills of southern South Carolina southward into the Atlantic coastal plain throughout most of Florida. It also ranges westward from the Florida panhandle along the Gulf coastal plain to extreme eastern Louisiana. They are still common in parts of their range, but are becoming rare in areas where they were once more abundant.

### Breeding Habits

Spring is the mating season for *Gopherus polyphemus*. The male displays an elaborate courtship by walking in a circle and periodically stopping to "bob" its head. Auffenberg (1966) calls this "the male orientation circle." Auffenberg theorized that the head-bobbing was to attract the attention of a sexually responsive female. Once a female is attracted, the male "bobs" his head more violently, then aggressive biting begins. He bites at her

head, forelegs and especially the gular projection. This usually triggers the female's mating urge and she backs in a semicircle, then stops to await the male. At this point mating usually takes place.

Photo by Nicholas Willis

*Male "gophers" have a conc[...] plastron and enlarged tail w[...] the cloaca extending past the e[...] of the marginals. Females ha[...] a convex plastron and short, th[...] tails. Mating takes place in t[...] spring.*

### Nesting and Egg-laying

Females begin nesting activity around late April, but some individuals nest as late as the end of July. The nests are constructed away from the burrows in most cases, but occasionally they are laid in the mound of sand at the entrance of the burrow.

The mouth of the nest is about four to five inches in diameter and the depth of the egg chamber is four and one-half to five inches. The hole is dug with alternate movements of the hind feet. The average clutch size is from four to seven eggs. Most gopher tortoise eggs are spherical with white, smooth, brittle shells. The eggs hatch during August and well into early September. Hatchlings measure about one and one-half inches and have pronounced yellow or orange spots on the center of each large shield on the carapace.

### Adult Behavior

*Gopherus polyphemus* are known for their burrowing propensities. They dig long, deep burrows which they use, in most cases, but not all, throughout their life. Some individuals may have a few alternate burrows which they occasionally use within their home-range territory. Burrows are almost always dug in sandy soil with the entrance being dry with good drainage, but the lowest portion, the terminal chamber, is usually somewhat moist. Most tortoise burrows are quite long, from fifteen to twenty-five feet. Hansen (1963) reported finding a gopher burrow forty-seven and a half feet long. The burrows of the gopher tortoise provide shelter for many other animals, some live in close association with the tortoises such as the gopher frog, *Rana capito,* while others may use it as temporary quarters. Among the mammals that have been found in "gopher holes" are raccoons, skunks, red foxes, rabbits, opossums, mice and rats. Quail and burrowing owls are two kinds of birds that use their burrows and a number of reptiles and amphibians have been observed in their holes. Some of these are: diamondback rattlesnakes, *Crotalus adamanteus,* indigo snakes, *Drymarchon corais couperi,* black racers, *Coluber con-*

Photo by Saul Friess

*he author examining a large ale gopher tortoise in the sand lls of southern South Carolina.*

*strictor priapus,* fence lizards, *Sceloporus undulatus undulatus,* broad-headed skink, *Eumeces laticeps,* glass lizard, *Ophisaurus ventralis* and the six-lined racerunner, *Cnemidophorus sexlineatus.* Aside from gopher frogs, the leopard frog, *Rana utricularia,* the southern toad, *Bufo terrestris,* and the eastern spadefoot toad, *Scaphiophus holbrook holbrooki* have also been found in the burrows of *Gopherus polyphemus.* Many arthropods occur in these burrows too. Some are there as obligates, while others are there as commensals. Young and Goff (1939) listed some thirty-two species of insects, spiders and ticks from "gopher" holes.

Most of my observations on *polyphemus* were made in the northernmost part of its range in South Carolina. These observations were carried out over several years and at various times of the year. The basking behavior seems to be well developed and this is usually done in the morning at the entrance of their burrow or on top of the sand mound. Most were seen basking with their heads in an elevated position and limbs folded to the sides. They are very wary, though, and will retreat down the burrow as fast as their stumpy legs will carry them at the slightest threat of danger. I have tried to pull large "gophers" out of the entrance of their hole without success. Once they are into the tunnel, they wedge themselves to the top and sides by extending the powerful front limbs. No amount of pulling will dislodge them unless one wishes to destroy the burrow by digging it out with a shovel. But my purpose was to observe the turtles, not remove them from their natural habitat. Gopher tortoises are highly specialized turtles and generally don't do well in captivity. Most soon starve themselves to death once they are taken from their burrows.

I only saw *Gopherus polyphemus* feeding in the wild on only one occasion. This was an adult female that was eating the fruit of the prickly pear cactus, *Opuntia spp.;* as well as the flowers and plant itself. On many of my walks through the sand hills of South Carolina where "gophers" occur, I saw great stands of *Opuntia* cacti growing along the edges of the oak and pine woods. Close examination of the cacti revealed the telltale bites left by the "gophers" that had been feeding on the plants. They are also known to eat mushrooms, various grasses and wild flowers. Carr (1952) examined the digestive tracts of wild gopher tortoises and found they contained the following items: large amounts of grass and leaves, some bits of hard fruits, bones, charcoal, and one specimen had the remains of insects (chitin).

Photo by James Bockowski

*prickly pear cactus,* Opuntia
*pp., with its pretty yellow flower*
*bloom. This is a favorite food of*
*e gopher tortoise.*

Local residents informed me that occasionally they find
gopher tortoises in their vegetable gardens, feeding on the to-
matoes and other vegetables.

### General Discussion

These are interesting and important animals in the coastal
plain environment. Their burrows serve as shelters for many
kinds of mammals, birds, reptiles and amphibians as well as
some invertebrates.

Gopher turtles are occasionally eaten in some parts of the

Photo. by Saul Frie

*An adult female gopher baskin at the edge of her burrow in th morning sun.*

South and they still are collected and sold in the pet trade. This reptile should be protected from mass habitat destruction before populations get dangerously low. Many are killed on highways as they endeavor to cross.

More recently, large numbers of *polyphemus* are being killed by rattlesnake hunters. Gas is poured down the burrow to drive the snakes out; once the snake comes up, the tortoises are left to die. This inhuman practice should be stopped. Not only are the rattlesnakes being mistreated by gassing, but all the other animals sharing the burrow with the snakes and turtles suffer as well.

# Chapter 8

# SEA TURTLES

Belonging to family *Cheloniidae* are some of the largest marine turtles known to science. Some attain weights up to 900 pounds or more. Marine turtles differ drastically from our freshwater turtles in many ways; a major difference, however, is their limbs. Sea turtles have well-developed flippers instead of true toes with claws. They have short necks and lack the ability to retract the head into the shell. The carapace is large, somewhat heart-shaped, and is covered with horny shields.

Their powerful paddle-shaped limbs serve well for locomotion in their totally aquatic environment. Once they emerge from the nest as hatchlings, and make their way across the beach to the water, they almost never come ashore again. Males rarely ever leave the safety of the water. Adult females only come ashore to deposit their eggs at the ancestral nesting grounds, but aside from that they, too, lead an entirely aquatic existence.

Most marine turtles are hunted by man as a food source. One species in particular has suffered greatly because of the delicious flavor of its flesh, this is the green turtle, *Chelonia mydas*. All other species are also eaten, but none are in as great a demand as the green turtle. As a result, its world population has become dangerously low.

The family *Cheloniidae* has four living genera and six species

found throughout the tropical seas of the world. In the United States are five species that occur in the warm coastal oceans; these are:

Photo by Saul F

*A large Alantic loggerhe Caretta caretta caretta. No its powerfull paddle-like flipp an adaptation for a totally aqu life at sea.*

1. The Green Sea Turtles; two subspecies are recognized: (Genus: *Chelonia)*
   A. Atlantic Green Turtle,
      *Chelonia mydas mydas*
   B. Pacific Green Turtle,
      *Chelonia mydas agassizi*
2. The Hawksbill Sea Turtles; two subspecies have been described. (Genus: *Eretmochelys)*
   A. Atlantic Hawksbill,
      *Eretmochelys imbricata imbricata*
   B. Pacific Hawksbill,
      *Eretmochelys imbricata bissa*
3. The Loggerhead Sea Turtles; there are two subspecies. (Genus: *Caretta)*
   A. Atlantic Loggerhead,
      *Caretta caretta caretta*

Photo by Saul Friess

*head shot of an Atlantic green rtle,* Chelonia mydas mydas. *It now considered an endangered ecies, because it has been hunted much by man as a food source.*

B.  Pacific Loggerhead,
    *Caretta caretta gigas*
4. The Ridley Sea Turtles, two species recently have been described (Genus: *Lepidochelys)*
A.  Atlantic Ridley, *Lepidochelys kempi*
B.  Indo-Pacific Ridley, *Lepidochelys olivacea*

The behavior and breeding habits of most marine turtles have been well documented in the literature by several authors, some

Photo by Saul Friess

*e Atlantic loggerhead,* Caretta retta caretta *occasionally nes into the waters off of Long land and Staten Island, New rk.*

of whom are world authorities on sea turtles, such as Archie Carr (1952), Peter Pritchard (1967) and Ernst and Barbour (1972), to name but a few. No attempt will therefore be made to give any of the sea turtles' habits here. The reader particularly interested in marine turtles is referred to the excellent accounts given by the authors mentioned above.

# LEATHERBACK SEA TURTLE
(Family *Dermochelyidae*)

The family *Dermochelyidae* is unique for two reasons; not only is it composed of a single living species, the leatherback *(Dermochelys coriacea),* but it can be said that the family also has the largest living reptile known to science. The "leathery turtle" as they are sometimes referred to, is found in all tropical oceans and may wander into temperate waters as well. They have been found as far north as New England and Canada. Leatherbacks are occasionally caught at sea in cool, northern oceans.

The "leathery turtle" lacks the horny carapacial shields found in other sea turtles. The elongated carapace is covered instead with a thick, leathery, oily skin. Embedded in the skin is a mosaic of hundreds of small separate bones.

## Size and Body Structure

The leatherback is the largest of all marine turtles. The average size specimens have carapace lengths of 50 to 70 inches and weights of 650 to 1300 pounds. Conant (1958) gives weights of 700 to 1500 pounds, and states: "They could possibly reach a ton." Ernst and Barbour (1972) relate, "There is some evidence that in the past individuals may have weighed a ton."

Pritchard (1971) obtained data on the measurements of 192 mature female leatherbacks from French Guiana. These ranged in size from 54 inches (the smallest individual), to specimens up to 71 inches (the largest of the group). About 100 of these had carapacial lengths that varied from 61 to 64 inches.

The streamlined carapace has seven prominent longitudinal ridges that divide it into eight sections and there are five keel-like ridges on the hingeless plastron. They have very large, powerful fore-flippers that are paddlelike in shape and lack claws entirely. The hind flippers are small and used mostly as balancers and for steering. The head is enormous with the upper jaw margin bear-

Photo by Wayne Frair

*carapace and the plastron*
*shields, but are covered in-*
*d by smooth leathery skin.*
*re five ridges on the lower*
*ion of the body and seven*
*itudinal ridges on the cara-*

ing two toothlike projections which are flanked by deep cusps. The snout is pointed with the nostrils situated at the tip for easy surface breathing. Males differ from females in that they have concave plastrons, a more streamlined carapace posteriorly, and long, thick tails that are longer than their rear flippers.

## Coloration

Leatherbacks usually have a dark brown or black carapace that is covered with numerous bluish-white or pinkish-white spots. In

most cases, the head and neck have spots that are larger than the
ones on the back. The plastron, undersides of the flippers, and
soft, fleshy ventral parts are pinkish-white and strongly marked
with a black, bluish or purplish marbled pattern.

### Range

*Dermochelys coriacea* has an almost worldwide distribution,
being found in all tropical seas and on occasion they wander into
temperate waters as well. They have been seen as far north as
Nova Scotia. In the United States they have been sighted off the
coastal waters of both the Atlantic and Pacific Oceans. There are
even records of leatherbacks nesting on beaches in Florida, but
this is a rare occurance.

### Breeding Habits

The actual courtship and mating of the leathery turtle has rarely
been observed. It is believed, however, that it takes place in the
waters off the coast of the nesting beaches, prior to or early in the
egg laying season.

### Nesting and Egg-laying

Nesting and egg-laying has been observed on beaches around the
world and in such faraway places as East and West Africa, South-
east Asia (Malaysia and Thailand), New Guinea, South America,
the Caribbean, Central America and Mexico.

It is probable that *Dermochelys coriacea* nest more than once a
year. There is some strong evidence that confirms this. Zwinenberg (1974) gives this interesting account; a female leatherback
was seen by Ceylon fishermen nesting on a beach in Ceylon. This
same female, who was easily identified because she was missing
one of her flippers, returned to the same beach three months later
to deposit eggs again. Frair (1972) states: "There are perhaps
seven or eight layings in one season at ten-day intervals."

Most authorities agree that leatherbacks usually emerge from
the sea at night to deposit their eggs. Females crawl up on the
beach and start digging the nest hole when they are well up onto
dry sand, some distance from the water. First she endeavors to
conceal herself by digging a body pit. This is dug with all four
flippers and with some sideway movements of the shell until she
is partially below the surface of the sand. The egg pit itself is only

Photo by J.P. Schulz courtesy of
Wayne Frair

*The head of the leatherback is enormous, as are the front flippers both of which the turtle readily uses to defend itself when threatened or annoyed.*

dug with the clawless hind flippers. Once her legs can no longer reach the bottom of the nest chamber to scoop out sand, egg-laying begins.

About 50 to 150 spherical, soft white eggs are laid in the deep nest about three feet deep. When egg-laying is completed, the leatherback sweeps sand into the nest chamber with her hind flippers and covers the eggs. Once this is done, she endeavors to hide the nesting site with sand-throwing strokes of the powerful fore-flippers. Then she laboriously crawls back to the sea.

The eggs hatch in approximately sixty to seventy-five days. In order for the hatchlings to reach the top of the nest chamber they must wait until the bulk of their nest mates also have hatched. Then they all begin to scramble around the egg chamber at the same time, causing the upper sand to fall downward. The motion caused by the mass of turtles packs the sand below them down and loosens up the sand above them. Subsequently, the hatchlings rise upward towards the top of the chamber. Slowly they reach the surface and emerge out onto the beach, crawling towards the sea as fast as they can (Zwinenberg, 1974).

*General Discussion:*

Throughout their range most sea turtles are threatened with extinction and the leatherback ranks high on the list. Not much is known about its behavioral pattern, habits, and wanderings because they spend most of their time out in open seas or searching for their favorite food, jelly fish.

Hatchlings fall prey to a host of predators such as ghost crabs, crows, vultures, gulls, frigate birds, pigs, dogs, cats and monitor lizards. If they do manage to reach the water they are killed and eaten by octopi, rock cod and many other large fishes. The adults often are attacked by sharks and killer whales. Man is by far their worst enemy.

# Chapter 9

# SOFT-SHELLED TURTLES

The family *Trionychidae* has representatives occurring in Africa, Asia, Malaysia and North America. There are seven genera within the family which has some twenty-two living species.

Soft-shelled turtles often are referred to as "pancake" turtles because of the shape and color of their carapace. They are round, flat turtles with a soft, leathery shell-like covering that lacks scales or shields entirely. The neck is extremely long and the snout is equipped with a "snorkel-like" projection (the nostrils) on the tip. They have strong, large paddlelike limbs that have three claws on each foot. The front legs have some large scales on the outer surfaces, but these are soft and leathery like the carapace.

Although soft-shells are highly aquatic in habits, this is one turtle that would probably give the proverbial hare a good race. This turtle is able to run on land with astonishing speed and agility. Once in the water their strong, powerful legs can propel them with even greater speed than on land; they seem to glide through the water like a fish.

These are large, aquatic freshwater turtles of rivers, canals, lakes and streams. They seem to show a preference for soft, sandy or muddy bottoms in which they spend much of their time well concealed. Buried in this position, their long necks stretch up to the surface for breathing while the rest of them remains hidden beneath sand or mud.

There is but a single genus, *Trionyx,* in the United States. The genus contains four species, these are:

1. The Smooth Soft-Shells; two subspecies have been described.
    A. Midland Smooth Soft-Shell,
        *Trionyx muticus muticus*
    B. Gulf Coast Smooth Soft-Shell,
        *Trionyx muticus calvatus*
2. The Spiny Soft-Shells; six subspecies are recognized.
    A. Eastern Spiny Soft-Shell
        *Trionyx spiniferus spiniferus*
    B. Western Spiny Soft-Shell
        *Trionyx spiniferus hartwegi*
    C. Gulf Coast Spiny Soft-Shell
        *Trionyx spiniferus asperus*
    D. Pallid Spiny Soft-Shell
        *Trionyx spiniferus pallidus*
    E. Guadalupe Spiny Soft-Shell
        *Trionyx spiniferus guadalupensis*
    F. Texas Spiny Soft-Shell
        *Trionyx spiniferus emoryi*
3. Florida Soft-Shell, *Trionyx ferox*
4. Chinese Soft-Shell, *Trionyx sinensis*
        (introduced into the Hawaiian Islands)

The member of this genus most familiar to me is the Florida Soft-Shell. It is a species I have seen in the field on a number of occasions and kept successfully in captivity as well.

# FLORIDA SOFT-SHELL TURTLE
(*Trionyx ferox*)

*Size and Body Structure*

*Trionyx ferox* is the largest of the American soft-shells. However, there is a considerable size difference between the sexes, females being by far the largest. They attain carapacial lengths from eight to nineteen inches. The smaller-sized males range from six to eleven and one half inches.

One of the most outstanding characteristics of this species is the presence of a marginal ridge around the upper edge of the leathery carapace. The anterior edge of the shell has numerous clusters of small bumps or knobby tubercles. The plastron is rather flat and the underlying bony structure can often be seen through the thin, tough skin. The legs are strong and muscular and each foot is equipped with well-developed webbing. The snout is long and tubular with a ridge on each nostril and the lips are thick and fleshy. A light line passes through each eye and sometimes extends onto the sides of the head and neck.

## Coloration

The typical appearance of *Trionyx ferox* is that of a dark brown or brownish-gray turtle on the upper surfaces with a vague sugges-

Photo by Zigmund Leszczynski

*arge adult female Florida soft-
ll, Trionyx ferox, floating on
surface of the water. This
cies is one of the largest soft-
lls in the United States, yet it
bably has the smallest range.*

tion of large markings or spots scattered irregularly about the
carapace. The plastron may have a few dark markings along the
posterior marginal end, but the rest is plain yellowish-white. The
pattern on the carapace is more pronounced on young individuals
and hatchlings.

Photo by Saul Frie

*An adult male Florida softshe
is basking on reeds at the edge (
a canal.*

### Range

As their name implies, the Florida Soft-Shell turtle occurs
throughout most of the state of Florida with the exception of the
western portion of the panhandle and the keys. It is also found in
southeastern South Carolina through southern Georgia.

# Chapter 10

# CARE OF PET TURTLES AND TORTOISES

Keeping turtles as pets has been a popular pastime among people of all ages for many years. Most families usually keep small aquatic species bought at a local pet store. Others may find a turtle as it crosses a road or capture one in a local pond or lake. Regardless of how the turtle is obtained, everyone is confronted with the same problem, and that's how to properly care for it and keep it healthy. Proper care of pet turtles can be placed in three main categories:

(1) Temperature
(2) Housing
(3) Diet

If these three requirements are properly met with there is no reason why a pet turtle cannot be kept in a home collection, alive and healthy, for many years.

## TEMPERATURE

Because turtles, like all reptiles, are cold-blooded animals and cannot maintain a constant body temperature of their own, it becomes necessary to provide a constant source of heat for them. Aquatic forms can be maintained in deep water at a steady temperature with the aid of an electric aquarium heater. However, care must be taken that the temperature is not allowed to go too high, as it may injure or kill the turtles in the tank. Shallow water species can be kept warm with a aquarium reflector light or a heat lamp. Always keep a thermometer inside a cage or on the side of the tank at all times so the temperature can easily be checked. In order for a turtle to function normally and feed properly they must be kept at an optimum temperature level. Most North American species do best at a temperature range of 75° to 85° F. If a turtle is allowed to become to cold or exposed to cold drafts they will go off food and will have great difficulty digesting any food already in their stomach. Aside from that, cool temperature will also cause a respiratory infection as well.

## HOUSING

Knowing something about a turtle's behavior and daily habits in the wild will certainly help one to set up its cage or tank properly. Some turtles are almost totally aquatic and spend little time basking. Others are basically aquatic, but spend several hours a day basking, whereas some are semi-aquatic and spend equal amounts of time on land and in the water. A few species are totally terrestrial and spend almost their entire life on land. Just knowing these simple facts and the type of environment they require could mean the difference between keeping a turtle successfully or not. Aquatic turtles are best housed in large glass aquarium tanks that must be kept clean. A ramp or platform must be provided to enable the turtles to easily climb up out of the water and dry off. The reflector light should be positioned so it is directly above the basking platform. Basking is extremely important to most turtles for many reasons. Lack of direct sunlight is a serious matter to most turtles who derive vitamin D by basking in the sun. If direct sunlight is not available (that is, sunlight that's not coming through glass; glass filters out the ultraviolet rays as well as vitamin D), then a good source of artificial light should be provided. Improper light may also hamper the turtles' feeding habits as well. If artificial light only is being used, it's best to use a wide spectrum artificial light such as Vita-lite made by the Duro-test Corporation, North Bergen, New Jersey. In the wild, aquatic turtles are able to free themselves of leeches by basking for hours in the rays of the sun. The leeches must drop off or they will dehydrate. Turtles belonging to the *Chrysemys* complex derive other benefits when shedding the plates off their shell. While basking, the heat of the sun dries the shields and peels them off the carapace.

Box turtles and tortoises can be housed in aquarium tanks or homemade wooden cages. The floor of the cage can be lined with #3 uncolored gravel, fine pine chips or just plain newspaper. Keeping the enclosure clean is of the utmost importance; gravel and wood chips can be kept clean by scooping out stools with an old tablespoon. Newspaper can be rolled up, thrown away and then replaced. Although unattractive, newspaper is probably the easiest and most sanitary cage lining one could use in keeping tortoises.

## DIET

Again familiarity with turtle behavior and feeding habits in the wild is a most important factor and reflects on how well one is able to keep them in captivity. Most turtles in their natural habitat have various periods of activity during the course of a day. This is governed by temperature, humidity and other environmental factors, but most wake early and bask until their body temperature is warm enough to allow foraging for food. Once enough food has been taken, the turtle returns to one of its favorite basking places to digest its meal. In captivity a turtle should be offered some of the foods it would normally eat in the wild, along with some supplementary items as well. Most importantly, never feed turtles in dirty water. Some hobbiests feed their turtle in a separate feeding bowl; this helps to keep the regular tank clean. A turtle's tank that does not have a filter should be cleaned at least every other day.

Most North American turtles have an omnivorous diet. That is, they feed on both plant and animal matter, therefore an assortment of meats, fish, fruits and vegetables should be offered to captive turtles. The following items are foods I have fed to pet turtles from time to time with a great deal of success:

(1)  Chopped or whole fish (don't use oily kinds of fish such as smelt or mackerel) too often
(2)  Chopped or whole shrimp
(3)  Chopped clams
(4)  Small snails (both land and aquatic types)
(5)  Crayfish
(6)  Tadpoles and frogs
(7)  Earthworms
(8)  Insects (both land and aquatic types)
(9)  Small mammals (mice and other rodents)
(10) Small birds or fowl (chicken parts etc.)
(11) Various kinds of chopped meats (horse, beef, pork)

(12) Leafy green vegetables (spinach, kale, lettuce etc.)

(13) Most other vegetables

(14) Various fruits and berries

All too often, turtle collectors make the mistake of not feeding their pets enough. Some people only feed their turtles once a week; this could be dangerous to their health causing improper growth and shell development. Turtles should be fed small amounts every day, or large amounts every other day. Most captive turtles, even of the same species, will have different feeding habits. What one turtle likes the other may not, so it will become necessary to experiment to see what your particular turtle's preferences are. Most captive turtles will feed on one or more of the above listed food items. Always give a new specimen a week or so to adjust to its new quarters; if they still don't feed then they should be released back at the place where they were captured. If it's an exotic turtle purchased in a pet store, then keep trying to feed it and make sure to provide the proper heat, housing, and foods suggested above.

If for some reason a pet turtle or tortoise should become sick or stop eating or is injured in some way, check with a veterinarian.

# HERPETOLOGICAL SOCIETIES YOU MIGHT
# WISH TO JOIN
## (Amateur Societies)

Florida Herpetological Society
6641 Rivo Alto Avenue
Orlando, Florida 32809

Chicago Herpetological Society
1402 Iroquois Drive
Wildwood, Illinois 60030

Maryland Herpetological Society
2643 North Charles Street
Baltimore, Maryland 21218

New York Herpetological Society
P.O. Box 3946 Grand Central Station
New York, N.Y. 10017

Society for the Study of Amphibians and Reptiles
Morton Hall, Ohio University
Athens, Ohio 45701

**For the professional or serious-minded amateur:**

The Herpetologists' League
Herpetologica
c/o Crawford G. Jackson, Jr.
San Diego Natural History Museum
P.O. Box 1390
San Diego, California 92112


*American Society of Ichthyologists & Herpetologists*
Copeia
Division of Reptiles & Amphibians,
United States National Museum
Washington, D.C. 20560


A pamphlet entitled *"Opportunities for the Herpetologist"* can be obtained by writing to the Secretary, Division of Reptiles & Amphibians, U.S. National History Museum, Washington, D.C. 20560


*Society for the Study of Amphibians & Reptiles*
c/o Henri C. Seibert
S.S.A.R. Publications Secretary
Department of Zoology, Mortan Hall
Ohio University
Athens, Ohio 45701

# LIST OF PERTINENT HERPETOLOGICAL TERMS FOR CROCODILIANS AND TURTLES

ALVEOLAR SURFACE   the crushing surface of the jaw of a turtle.

ANTERIOR   before or toward the front.

BARBELS   small, fleshy downward projections from the chins and throats of turtles.

CARAPACE   the upper shell of a turtle.

CARUNCLE   eggtooth-like modification of skin on the snout of hatchling turtles.

CENTRALS   the median row of laminae of a turtle carpace.

CLINE   a gradual change in a variable characteristic.

CLOACA   a common chamber into which the digestive, excretory, and reproductive tracts empty. It opens to the outside through the vent.

CREPUSCULAR   active at twilight and/or dawn.

CUSP   a toothlike projection on the jaw of a turtle.

DORSAL   pertaining to the upper surface of the body.

DORSOLATERAL   pertaining to the upper sides.

DORSUM   the upper, or dorsal, surface.

ESTIVATION   a state of enactivity during prolonged periods of drought or high temperatures, usually while the animal is in seclusion.

EXFOLIATION   scaling off in flakes.

FORM   a species or a subspecies; a distinct, identifiable population.

FRONTAL   a single median plate on top of the head between the eyes.

GRAVID   bearing eggs or young, usually in the oviduct.

GROWTH RINGS   concentric subcircular areas on the scutes of some turtles. Each "ring" represents a seasons growth. Rings, if present, are most evident in young turtles; they are usually not countable in adults.

HYBRID   the offspring of the union of a male of one race, variety, species, genus, etc., with the female of another.

INFRAMARGINALS   short rows of laminae between the plastrals and marginals in a turtle shell.

INTERGRADE   to merge gradually one with another through a series of intermediate forms.

INTERNAL NARES   the openings of the nasal passages in the roof of the mouth.

INTERNASAL   one or two scales on top of the head just behind the rostral.

INTERPARIETAL   a single median scale on the head behind the frontal. It may be seperated from the latter by the paired frontoparietals.

JUVENILE   a young or immature individual, often displaying proportions and coloration differing from that of the adult.

KEEL   a longitudinal ridge on the scales of certain lizards and snakes or down the back or venter of a turtle.

LABIALS   (upper and lower) scales bordering the jaw.

LAMINAE   the scales of a turtle's shell.

LATERALS   the row of enlarged laminae on each side of the centrals on a turtle's shell.

MANDIBLE   the lower jaw of a turtle.

MARGINALS   the laminae forming the edge of a turtle's shell.

MAXILLARY   pertaining to the upper jaw.

MELANISM   abundance of black pigment, sometimes resulting in an all-black or nearly all-black animal; opposite of albinism.

MICROENVIRONMENT   the immediate surrounding of an organism.

MIDDORSAL   of or pertaining to the center of the back.

MIDVENTRAL   of or pertaining to the center of the abdomen.

NASAL   the scale in which the nostril lies.

OCELLUS   (pl. ocelli) a small eye; and eyelike spot.

OVIPAROUS   producing eggs that hatch after laying.

OVUM   a female germ cell; an egg cell or egg apart from any investing membrane.

PAPILLAE   small nipplelike protuberances.

PARAVERTABRAL STRIPE a stripe to one side and parallel to the dorsal midline.

PECTORALS   pertaining to the chest. The second paired luminae on the plastron of a turtle.

PEDUNCLE   a stem or stalk.

PHALANGES   the bones of the toes.

PLASTRALS   the laminae covering the plastron.

PLASTRON   the lower shell of a turtle.

POSTCENTRALS   the pair of marginals immediately posterior to the last central in turtles.

POSTERIOR   situated behind or to the rear.

PRECENTRAL   the single unpaired laminae preceding the centrals.

PREFRONTALS   one or two pairs of scales on top of the head in front of the frontal.

PREOCULAR   one or more small scales directly in front of the eye.

RACE   subspecies.

RELICT   a survivor, especially of a vanishing race, type, or species; belonging to a nearly extinct class.

ROSTRAL   plate at the tip of the snout.

SCUTE   any enlarged scale on a reptile; sometimes called a "plate."

SEAM   the furrow seperating the laminae of the shell of a turtle.

SERRATE saw-toothed.

SHIELD   in turtles, any one of the plates of horn that cover the shell.

SIBLING SPECIES   two or more species that have derived from a common parental stock. They often resemble each other closely and replace one another geographically; their ranges may or may not overlap at points of contact.

SUBOCULARS   scales between the eye and the labials.

SUBMARGINALS   a few small scales between the marginals and the plastrals of the alligator snapping turtle.

SUBSPECIES   a subdivision of a species; a variety or race; a category (usually the lowest category recognized in classification) ranking next below a species.

SUPRALABIALS   scales along the lower margin of the upper jaw—the lip scales.

SUPRAOCULARS   scales above the eyes.

SUPRAORBITAL RIDGES   ridges above the eyes.

TEMPORALS   scales, lying one above the other, behind the postocular and between the parietals and upper labials.

TEMPORALS, ANTERIOR   one or two longitudinal, elongated scales, lying one above the other, behind the postoculars and between the parietals and upper labials.

TIBIA   the leg portion from heel to knee.

TOMIUM   the horny covering of the jaws in turtles.

TUBERCLE(S)   a small knoblike projection.

TUBERCULATE   with raised projections.

TYMPANUM   the eardrum.

VENT   the opening on the surface of the body of the cloaca which in reptiles and amphibians is the common chamber into which the intestinal, urinary and reproductive canals discharge.

VENTER   the belly or underside of an animal.

VENTRAL   the underside, or lower surface, of the body.

VERTEBRAL LINE OR STRIPE   a stripe down the midline of the back, overlying the position of the vertebral column.

VERTICAL PUPIL   an elliptical pupil with its long axis vertical.

(This glossary was compiled from the following sources: Conant (1958, 1975) Stebbins (1966) and Cochran and Goin (1970).

# LIST OF ECOLOGICAL TERMS

ADAPTATION   any characteristic which helps an organism to survive in its particular environment.

BALANCE IN NATURE   tendency of living things to maintain a dynamic equilibrium between themselves and their environment.

CARNIVORE   a secondary consumer; an animal that feeds on other animals.

COMMUNITY   an interrelated and interdependent group of plants and animals.

CONSUMER   in the food chain, all organisms other than green plants.

DECAY   reduction of the materials of plants or animal bodies to simple compounds through the action of bacteria or other decomposers.

DECOMPOSERS   organisms that break down tissues and excretion of other organisms into simpler forms; bacteria, yeast, mold and other fungi, etc.

ECOLOGY   study of the relationship of living things including man, to each other and to their environment.

ENERGY   the ability to do work.

ENVIRONMENT   all of the biological and physical components of a given place.

EROSION   loss of water caused by the action of wind and water.

FOOD CHAIN   transfer of energy through an ecosystem through the action of food producers, food consumers, and decomposers.

HABITAT   the place where a plant or animal can find the right food, shelter, water, temperature, and other things it needs to live.

HERBIVORE   a plant-eating animal; a primary consumer.

HUMUS   organic material in soil, produced by plant and animal decomposition.

INTERRELATIONSHIP   the interaction between plants and animals and their environment.

NICHE   the "job" a living thing does; its relation to its environment.

PREDATOR   an animal that preys on other animals.

PRODUCER   in the food chains green plants; the only organisms capable of making food.

RESPIRATION   exchange of gases (oxygen in; carbon dioxide out) between living cells (plant and animal) and the environment, including oxidation and the release of energy.

TRANSPIRATION   loss of water from plants into the surrounding environment.

WATER CYCLE   continuous movement of water, in its various forms, between earth and air.

(Glossary based on the one in A Place To Live—Educational Services, National Audubon Society.)

# Literature Cited

Arndt, Rudolf G. 1972. Additional records of *Clemmys Muhlenbergi* in Delaware. Bull. Maryland Herp. Society 8 (1): pp. 1-5.

Auffenberg, W. On the courtship of *Gopherus Polyphemus*. Herpetologica 22: 113-117.

Barton, A.J. and J.W. Price. 1955. Our knowledge of the bog turtle, *Clemmys muhlenbergi*. Copeia 1955 (3): 159-165.

Babcock, Harold L. 1919. Turtles of New England. Memoirs of the Boston Society of Natural History, 8: 323-431.

Behler, John L. 1970. The bog turtle, *Clemmys muhlenbergi* in Monroe County, Pennsylvania. Bull. Maryland Herp. Society 6 (3): 52-53.

———. 1971. The Bog Turtle, *Clemmys Muhlenbergi*. Animal Kingdom, inside cover.

Bellairs, Angus. 1970. *The Life Of Reptiles*. New York: Universe Books. 2 vols.

Bloomer, Tom J. and Denise Bloomer. 1973. New Jersey's bog turtle. . . .destined to extinction? Bull. N.Y. Herp. Society 9 (3&4): 8-12.

Bowler, Kevin J. 1972. Crocodilians: a profile. America's First Zoo, Philadelphia Zoological Garden (24) 3: 18-21.

Brazaitis, Peter. 1967. Endangered! Animal Kingdom. 122-127.

———. 1968. Crocodilian pets. New York: New York Zoological Society.

———. 1968. The Chinese alligator. Animal Kingdom pp. 24-27.

Carr, A.F. 1952 *Handbook of Turtles*. Ithaca, N.Y.: Comstock Publ. Assoc.

———. 1963. *The Reptiles*. New York: Time, Inc.

———. 1940. A Contribution to the herpetology of Florida. University of Florida Biological Science 3: pp. 1-118.

Clement Herbert. 1968. Turns of the turtles. Animaland 35 (4) p. 1.

Cochran, Doris M. and Coleman J. Goin. 1970. *The New Field Book of Reptiles and Amphibians*. New York: G.P. Putnam's Sons.

Conant, Roger. 1957. Reptiles and amphibians of the northeastern United States. Philadelphia: Zoological Society of Philadelphia.

———. 1958. *A Field Guide To Reptiles and Amphibians*. 1st edition. Boston: Houghton Mifflin.

———. 1975. *A Field Guide to Reptiles and Amphibians of Eastern and Central North America*. 2nd editiion, Boston: Houghton Mifflin.

Davis, W.T. 1928. Natural history records from the meetings of the Staten Island Nature Club. Proc. Staten Island Institute of Arts and Science 4: 116-123.

Degenhardt, William G. and James L. Christianson. 1974. Distribution and Habits of Turtles in New Mexico. The Southwestern Naturalist. 19 (1): 21-46.

DeKay, James E. 1842. Zoology of New York or the New York Fauna. Albany: White & Visscher. (Plate 8, Figure 15).

Ditmars, R.L. 1907. *The Reptile Book*. N.Y.: Doubleday, Page & Company.

———. 1936. *The Reptiles of North America*. Garden City, New York: Doubleday and Company.

———. 1933. *Reptiles of the World*. New York: Macmillan, pp. 321.

Eglis, Arsene, 1967. *Clemmys muhlenbergi,* rarest of North American turtles. Animal Kingdom (70): p. 58-61.

Ernst, Carl H. and Roger W. Barbour. 1972. *Turtles of the United States*. Lexington, Kentucky: University Press of Kentucky.

Frair, Wayne. 1972. Serology of turtles. Copeia. 1: pp. 97-108.

———. 1963. Blood group studies with Turtles. Science. 3574: pp. 1412-1414.

———. Leatherback: northward ho! Aquasphere. 6 (3): p. 13.

Frair, Wayne, Ackman R.G. and Mrosovsky N. 1972. Body Temperature of *Dermochelys coriacea:* Warm Turtle from Cold Water. Science. 177: pp. 791-793.

Frair, Wayne, Stephen Cook and Donald Abb. 1972. A new record size box turtle. International Turtle and Tortoise Society Journal. 6 (3).

Frye, Frederic L. 1974. Husbandry, medicine, and surgery in captive reptiles. Bonner Springs, Kansas: VM Publishing Inc.

Gibbons, J.W. Observations on the ecology and population dynamics of the Blanding's turtle, *Emydoidea blandingi*. Canadian Journal of Zoology 46: 288-90.

Goin, Coleman J. and Olive B. 1971. *Introduction to Herpetology*. 2nd edition. San Francisco: W.H. Freeman.

———. 1972. *Family Sphenodontidae*. Introduction to Herp.

Guggisberg, C.A.W. 1972. *Crocodiles.* Harrisburg: Stackpole.

Holbrook, Dr. John E. 1836. *North American Herpetology: A Description of the Reptiles Inhabiting the United States.* Philadelphia: Dobson.

Huheey, James E. and Arthur Stupka. 1967. *Amphibians and Reptiles of Great Smoky Mountains National Park* Knoxville, Tenn.: University of Tennessee Press.

Kauffeld, Carl F. 1955. *Pet Alligators.* Fond du lac: All-Pets Books, Inc.

———. 1949. *Staten Island Turtles.* Animaland. 16 (2): p. 4.

———. 1972. Snapping turtles. Animaland. 39 (1): p. 5.

King, Wayne F., Manuel Rubio, et al. 1970. The American Alligator. Bull. New York Herp. Society 6: 2-40.

Legler, J.M. 1955. Observations on the sexual behavior of captive turtles. Lloydra. 18: pp. 95-99.

Leng, C.W. and W.T. Davis. 1930. *Staten Island and Its People: A History.* 1609 - 1929. Vol. 5. New York: Lewis Hist. Publ. Co.

McDowell, Samuel B. 1964. Partition of the genus *Clemmys* and related problems in the taxonomy of the aquatic testudinidae. Proc. Zool. Soc. London 143: 229-279.

Mathewson, R.F. 1955. Reptiles and amphibians of Staten Island. Proc. Staten Island Inst. Arts, and Sciences. Staten Island Museum Pub.

Minton, Sherman A. and Madge Rutherford Minton, 1973. *Giant Reptiles.* Charles Scribner's Sons, New York.

Neill, Wilfred T. 1971. *The Last of the Ruling Reptiles: Alligators, Crocodiles, and their Kin.* New York: Columbia University Press.

Nemuras, Kenneth T. 1966. Genus *clemmys*. International Turtle & Tortoise Society. J. 1 (1): 26-27, 39, 44.

———. 1967. Genus *clemmys*. International Turtle & Tortoise Society. J. 1 (2): 38-40.

———. 1967. Notes on the natural history of *Clemmys muhlenbergi*. Bull. Maryland Herp. Society. 3: 80-96.

———. 1968. Again, the spotted turtle. International Turtle & Tortoise Society. J. 2 (3): 32-35.

———. 1969. Survival of the muhlenberg. International Turtle & Tortoise Society. J. 3 (5): 18-21.

———. 1974. The bog turtle. Wild Life in North Carolina.

Ogden John C. 1973. Night of the crocodile. Audubon. 75: 32-37.

Pope. C.H. 1946. *Turtles of the United States and Canada.* New York: Knopf.

Pritchard, Peter C.H. 1967. *Living Turtles of the World.* Jersey City: T.F.H. Publications.

Pritchard, C.H. The leatherback or leathery turtle. Morges: I.U.N.C., monograph no. 1.

Richard, Maurice L. 1972. *The Fascination of Reptiles.* New York: Hill and Wang.

Romer, Alfred S. 1956. *Osteology of the Reptiles.* Chicago: Univ. of Chicago.

Schmidt, Karl P. and Robert F. Inger. 1957. *Living Reptiles of the World.* Garden City, N.Y.: Doubleday and Co.

Schoepff, Dr. Johann D. 1792-1801. Historia testudinum naturge-schichte der schildkroten. Erlanger: J.J. Palm.

Sharell, Richard. 1966. *The Tuatara, Lizards and Frogs of New Zealand.* London: Collins.

Smith, Hobart M. 1956. *Handbook of Amphibians and Reptiles of Kansas.* Univ. Kansas Mus. Nat. Hist. Misc. Publ. 9: 1-356.

Vogel, Zdenek. 1964. *Reptiles and Amphibians, Their Care and Behavior.* New York: The Viking Press.

Weaver, W.G. and F.L. Rose. 1967. Systematics, fossil history, and evolution of the genus *Chrysemys.* Tulane Stud. Zool. 14: 63-67.

Wermuth, H., and Mertens, 1961. *Schildkroten, Krokodile, Brunckeneschen.* Jena: Verlag.

Young, F.N., and Goff, CC. An annotated list of arthropods found in the burrows of the Florida gopher tortoise, *Gopherus polyphemus.* Florida Entomology 12: 53-62.

Zappalorti, Robert T. 1968. Through the greenbelt, (S.I. turtles). International Turtle and Tortoise Society Journal, p. 35-39.

———. 1973. To save a turtle, *Clemmys muhlenbergi.* Phila. Herp. Society, News Bulletin.

———. 1973. Progress report to National Audubon Society on bog turtle Research, p. 4, 20. (unpublished).

———. 1975. The status of the bog turtle, *Clemmys muhlenbergi,* in North Carolina with some notes on its behavior and breeding habits. Special publication of the Highlands Museum and Biological Station.

Zug. G.R. 1966. The penial morphology and the relationships of cryptodiran turtles. Occ. Pap. Mus. Zool. Univ. Michigan. 647: 1-24.

Zwinenberg, A.J. 1974. The leatherback. Bull. Maryland Herpetological Society. 10 (2): 42.

Zwinenberg A.J. 1975. The green turtle *(Chelonia mydas),* one of the reptiles most consumed by man, needs immediate protection. Bull. Maryland Herp. Society. 11 (2).

# METRIC CONVERSION TABLE

The numbers in the central column refer to the measurement either in centimeters or inches which are to be converted. If converting from inches to centimeters, the equivalent will be found in the column on the left, while if converting from centimeters to inches, the answer will be found in the column on the right.

| Centimeters | | Inches |
|---|---|---|
| 2.5 | 1 | .4 |
| 5.0 | 2 | .8 |
| 7.5 | 3 | 1.2 |
| 10.0 | 4 | 1.6 |
| 12.5 | 5 | 2.0 |
| 25.0 | 10 | 4.0 |
| 50.0 | 20 | 8.0 |
| 75.0 | 30 | 12.0 |
| 100.0 | 40 | 16.0 |
| 125.0 | 50 | 20.0 |

To convert measurements not shown on the table:
Inches into centimeters: Multiply the number of inches by 2.5.
Example: Convert 8 inches into centimeters.
        8 x 2.5 = 20 cm.
Centimeters into inches: Divide the number of centimeters by 2.5.
Example: Convert 13 centimeters into inches.
        13 ÷ 2.5 = 5.2 in.

# TEMPERATURE CONVERSION TABLE

The numbers in the central column refer to the temperature either in degrees centigrade or Fahrenheit which are to be converted. If converting from degrees Fahrenheit to centigrade, the equivalent will be found in the column on the left, while if converting from degrees centigrade to Fahrenheit, the answer will be found in the column on the right.

| Centigrade | | Fahrenheit |
|---|---|---|
| −28.9 | −20 | −4 |
| −23.3 | −10 | 14 |
| −17.8 | 0 | 32 |
| −12.2 | 10 | 50 |
| − 6.67 | 20 | 68 |
| − 1.11 | 30 | 86 |
| 4.44 | 40 | 104 |
| 10.0 | 50 | 122 |
| 15.6 | 60 | 140 |
| 21.1 | 70 | 158 |
| 23.9 | 75 | 167 |

| 26.7 | 80 | 176 |
| 29.4 | 85 | 185 |
| 32.2 | 90 | 194 |
| 35.0 | 95 | 203 |
| 36.7 | 98 | 208.4 |
| 37.8 | 100 | 212 |

For temperatures not shown:

Centigrade degrees into Fahrenheit degrees:

Multiply the number of centigrade degrees by 9/5 and add 32 to the result. Example: Convert 37°C into Fahrenheit degrees.

37 x 9/5 = 66.6     66.6 + 98.6°F

Fahrenheit degrees into centigrade degrees:

Subtract 32 from the number of Fahrenheit degrees and multiply the difference by 5/9. Example: Convert 212°F into centigrade.

212 − 32 = 180     180 x 5/9 = 100°C

# INDEX